Go Get 'Em, Tiger!

Becoming the Person You Want To Be

by Jimmy Weldon

First printing, May 1990
Second printing, January 1995
Third printing, August 2007

Printed by Delta Lithograph Co. in Valencia, CA

Jimmy Weldon Enterprises
5104 Ledge Avenue
Burbank, CA 91505-2724

Contents

Foreword

When I met Jimmy Weldon in 1989, I was about as motivated as a Chia Pet in debt. On one hand, I enjoyed the benefits of a successful automobile appraisal and inspection company. I was certified in my field and often provided expert witness testimony in unique court and arbitration cases. In fact, I still do.

But on the other hand, I was a prisoner to chronic neck and back pain that had been plaguing me for years. After fourteen physicians, three pain centers, and $130,000, a special kind of depression had set in. I basically felt as lost as one could feel yet still be alive.

Then along came Jimmy...

We both belong to the Mercedes-Benz Club of America, and Jimmy had just arrived at one of our monthly meetings in his new car. He was 30 years my senior and 60 times happier. As he walked in, someone said, "How are ya doin', Jimmy?" He replied, in a penetrating voice, "If I felt any better, I couldn't stand it."

That aforementioned exchange effectively ignited a spark in me that ultimately changed my life.

We met over dinner that evening, and within a few hours I found myself embracing his "Go Get 'Em, Tiger" concepts—and I now live a healthier, happier, and more productive existence.

Even without the pain, I had fallen victim to the negative environment we are so often born into. You know, your attitude and values get rusty. They need retooling—that is, if you truly intend to enjoy life.

As I've watched Jimmy grow (younger) through the years, I've observed this architect of life as he empowered students, educators, corporate executives, civic leaders and the general public with his personal appearances, books and tapes.

In this book, Jimmy talks about goal setting, and then shows you how to succeed in the real world by sharing some real world examples.

He explores the benefits of doing what you want to do, and explains how to make the necessary changes to make that possible. By following Jimmy's advice, you can learn to enjoy every day of your life to the fullest.

Jimmy is determined to *make* you succeed in your personal and professional life, just as he did with me, by stressing a new perspective.

Even though I feel you've struck it rich with this book, Jimmy will undoubtedly continue to drill for oil in the motivational field for years to come.

Ken Marchant

I have known the author for more than seventy-one years; therefore I can verify the opening statements of his book, because I was present at the time. In fact, I will go further and state that the entire contents are nothing but the truth.

When you read about the *early years*, I must admit his penning of events really tells it like it was. Bub and I would have gladly replaced him for another brother or sister, time and time again. I even began calling him Lummox— the definition of dumb ox, to be precise. Strangely, it stuck; and to this very day, that is the name he uses in reference to himself when he and I are writing or conversing... and I do, too. As for *little brothers*, I can say unequivocally, there could be no equal. I remember, about sixty years ago, one of his classmates said, "When they made Verne, they broke the mold."

As one of television's pioneers, Lummox has actually lived through its development, and you will laugh as you read of the experiences he has had. He has a zest for life that is contagious.

Every young person reading this book will find inspiration to follow the course of whatever it is they set their mind to do. It's good for all of us, regardless of our age.

The best description I can give of him is that he is like the little rabbit in today's commercials; he just keeps going and going and going....

It must be obvious that I love and am very proud of my baby brother. Enjoy his book now and as he says, "Go get 'em, Tiger!"

J. LaMoyne Shinn
Santa Margarita, California

Standing outside of the Little Church in the Pines, at Bass Lake California in 1962, is the only person who ever made me look *shy*... my father. You are going to know this man by the time you finish my book, and I believe you will love him as much as I do!

Special Thanks

I would especially like to thank George R. Hensel, who is the founder of the California Driving School, the largest facility of its kind. George believes so strongly in motivation and personal development of employees that he paid *all* expenses for fifty instructors to attend my four hour seminar, "The Leader in You."

A ndre Grieco, a young man I have known twenty-five years... a wonderful husband and father; someone I would have been proud to have had as my own son. He begged and pleaded with me to have a professional editor go over this manuscript, and I followed his advice.

T hat person, Kathy Kennel, is a walking word processor and has made my book readable—grammatically correct, that is. She is pure magic. (Oh, and by the way— she is also the National President of the Mercedes-Benz Club of America.)

L ast... my dear friend, Ken Marchant. Had it not been for his final 'okay' to take this to the printer, you would not have it in your hands now. And, after reading the foreword, you can appreciate his tremendous writing skills, even making me feel that I was... uh... nuf sed!

1. The Witnessed Murder

"Mama, he killed that little girl."

"What little girl?"

"Mama, I saw him. He killed her!"

"Babe, what in the world are you talking about?"

Almost sixty-four years have raced by since that little seven year old boy made those disturbing statements to his mother, who knelt down and tenderly wrapped her arms around him.

I had no idea what she was going to say would crystallize my future. *Yes, I was that little boy.*

Between sobs and outright hysteria, Mom gradually calmed me down with a loving hug, but her words were the most comforting.

"Babe, it was all play-like."

"Play-like?"

"Yes, Babe, play-like."

"But, Mama, I *saw* the bottle hit her in the head and the blood scattered everywhere."

"What you thought was blood, Babe, was probably ketchup." I could understand that. "And the little girl wasn't hurt, she was only acting."

"Only acting... what's that?"

You see, my two brothers had just brought me home from viewing a portion of the first movie I'd ever seen in my life, *Ten Nights In a Bar Room.*

The main character in this melodrama was the town drunk who spent most of his time in the local tavern. His little girl was looking for him and had walked down to the saloon, hoping he was there.

Just as the little girl came through the swinging doors, the bartender threw a beer bottle at her father and it accidentally hit her in the head.

Blood splattered everywhere, as she fell down on the floor. I remember putting my hands up to my head—I suppose it was a reaction of protecting myself—but then, I ran outside screaming!

Bub and Moyne were so embarrassed as they followed and took me home. I had no idea a movie was fiction. No one had explained that. I thought everything I had seen was real.

Although Mom had no knowledge of producing films, she could have been Darryl F. Zanuck the way she described how they were made, while I listened spellbound. She finally made me understand the beer bottle didn't hit the little girl; it only *looked* that way to us at the theatre. Gollleeeeeeee!

"They probably gave her a glass of milk and some cookies while waiting to film something else," she added, which made my eyes really open wide.

"I would have wanted some vanilla wafers if it had been me, Mom."

"I'm sure they have that kind too, Babe."

Wowweeee! I was sure some day *I* was going to do that. We giggled at how much fun and exciting acting must be, enjoying play-like adventures every day.

Movies... actors... drama... *cookies*... Hollywood... *having fun forever!*

I didn't grow up wanting to be a doctor one day, an attorney the next, a baseball player the following week, or some other childhood fantasy.

I knew precisely at that moment I was going to Hollywood and be in pictures; yet I didn't have the slightest idea where Hollywood was—or even the city limit signs in Chickasha, Oklahoma for that matter. I didn't care. I *knew* what I was going to do!

D ear friend, hidden in your mind—the last unexplored continent on earth—are memories, happy and sad. Memories you can dismiss by simply saying to yourself, 'I'm not going to think about that right now,' because your mind will only think about what you *permit it* to think about.

That's no ridiculous remark; it's a fact. You reserve the power to exercise absolute control over the most highly organized yet incredibly complicated entity in the world. *A computer with unlimited potential... your brain!*

Well... the very next morning, no longer afraid, I began my lifelong journey of being that actor in Hollywood. No, I didn't run up and down the road yelling what a great star I would be some day. I didn't even tell anyone what had become my dream—all from seeing that movie—but I went to every one I could. I watched carefully what each actor did and thought about how I would have played the roles. It was a whole new adventure with every film, and I loved them all.

Dad made me a little stick horse out of an old broom handle. I looped a piece of string through a hole he drilled in one end, and that served as my reins. I became the Lone Ranger, and the broom handle was Silver. I threw my left leg over that old wooden vestige and imagined I was climbing into the most beautiful saddle ever fashioned. I held that piece of string tightly in my right hand and, being left-handed, slapped my hip with the left one. The end of that old round piece of wood sliding across the ground left a wiggly trail in the dirt which, along with my galloping legs, formed clouds of dust whirling in the air *as I rode into the sunset.*

Before you split your sides laughing, remember... we didn't have any video games, television or other kinds of electronic entertainment.

Little Orphan Annie on the *radio* was our big thrill back in the 1930's. Television? What in the world was that?

Today our young people are born with a TV set in the room, and there are others scattered all over the house. I have seen little hand held "3-inchers" on sidewalks and beaches, in football stadiums and baseball bleachers. They are everywhere.

I believe what is basically wrong with today's parents is unrestricted television for the really young children. Some don't have the vaguest idea what their little ones are watching.

Parents no longer help their youngsters *just grow up.* They're too busy with their own lives, concentrating on what's considered urgent at the moment. Back in the years when I was at this impressionable age, Mom was my true companion. Every Saturday in the Midwest Theatre, we were perched on the edge of our seats watching a cowboy movie. (Well, at least *I* was.) I loved every minute of our time together, and that nickel bag of hot, buttered popcorn was soooooooo good, too.

The notion comes to mind that perhaps you bought this book from me personally after I had spoken somewhere. So many people had asked if I had ever written one, it finally *registered* that maybe I should do it.

But first, I want to sell you on three facts if I possibly can. You are the most important person in the world. You know more about yourself than all of the other people in the world combined... and **you are the only person you are never going to leave**.

It's up to you. You can do *anything* you want to if you *believe* you can.

Disraeli said it like this: "Everything comes if a man will only wait. I have brought myself by long meditation to the conviction that a human being with a settled purpose must accomplish it and that nothing can resist a will that will stake even existence for its fulfillment."

What a bunch of words to say, "I'll do it if it kills me." How *basic* can you get?

Now, if you and I believe those three facts, shouldn't everyone *else* feel that way? Our personal relationships have so much to do with that, as you will see later. For instance, how often do you use the two most important phrases anyone can hear: *Thank you* and *I love you*?

Please pretend we're sitting together and I'm telling you why I believe **becoming the person you want to be** should be taught to every young person and why it's so important.

This book explains how I'm doing what I wanted to do when I was a little boy, and how I'm still looking forward to accomplishing other dreams and goals at the *young* age of seventy-one.

This book also exposes the devastating, unseen killer, **complacency**, which will overtake you without warning and is far more destructive than you can imagine. I hope with all my heart these pages will make your life more meaningful and convince you of your uniqueness in all the world.

It's not what you say to people that counts; it's what they believe of what you say that really matters. I'm asking you to please be my jury and not turn in a verdict until all of the evidence is in. I promise you one thing: When you have completed this book, you'll say, "That ol' boy sure believes in what he says."

I was born September 23, 1923 in Dale, Texas... with a population of about one hundred. I have two older brothers. We are the Shinn boys: Joe Weldon, James Lamoyne and, believe it or not, me... Ivy Laverne. We call Joe Bub or Bubba. Lamoyne and I went by our middle names but dropped 'La,' so our schoolmates knew us as Moyne (rhymes with coin) and Verne.

We lived in small Texas communities until I was seven years old, when we moved to Chickasha (Chick-uh-shay), Oklahoma on Halloween night in 1930. Thirteen thousand people. Wow! *We had arrived!*

As Bub and Moyne were both athletes, I went to a lot of football and basketball games. But every time I sat with Mom and Dad on the sidelines, I honestly was more interested in watching the yell leaders. In fact, this fascination launched me in a *career* which began the last day of grammar school.

I bounced up in front of the room and announced, "We're going to give a yell for Miss Carrington, our teacher!" She was flabbergasted and so were my classmates, but I projected such self-confidence they jumped to their feet.

"Let's give 'Yea, Miss... Yea, Carrington... Yea, Yea... Miss Carrington'."

And we did!

She cried because no one had ever done that. Well, what class in grade school had ever shown a teacher affection by giving them a *yell*?

My classmates' response, plus Miss Carrington's overwhelming approval, gave me a new goal which I was determined to strive for the following year in junior high!

2. Child Abuse... *Innocently Administered*

I'm skipping ahead now to lay some ground work for material I will discuss later.

Just when I was gaining the confidence that my speaking ability would one day generate the major portion of my income, I addressed a group of dentists, orthodontists and dental surgeons in Fresno, California. I stressed the importance of teaching children the proper principals, but begged them never to say to a child, "This is what you're going to do when you grow up!" Instead, ask that child what he or she *wants* to do; and when they tell you, ask them if that is *really* what they want. If the answer is, "Yes, I'm sure it is," then agree with their choice and help them go after it. I believe with all my heart the words across the top of my business cards are undeniably true: *If thou canst believe, all things are possible to him that believeth*—Mark 9:23.

After finishing my presentation, I was still standing by the blackboard as most of those in the room were leaving for a break. A handsome young doctor who stayed behind shocked me as he softly declared, "Jimmy, you really hurt me today."

"I what?"

"Well, maybe not hurt me—helped me, perhaps."

"How is that, Doctor?"

"Jimmy, I live in a little town in Iowa; and, by all of the standards you wrote on the blackboard defining success, I am one of the most successful business men there. I have a great practice, a wonderful family and...." Suddenly he stopped, tears gathering in his eyes. He glanced at the floor closing each hand tightly into a fist, then looked up with a pained expression. "God... **I hate every day of my life!**"

I was stunned. "I don't understand, Doctor. What do you mean?"

"When I was three years old my father said, 'Son, you are going to be a dental surgeon because *I* am.' I didn't even understand what he meant. Everywhere we went he held my hand, announcing to his friends and colleagues, 'This is my little dental surgeon.'

"After I started school, I realized becoming a dental surgeon was not what I wanted to do; but I couldn't disappoint him—he was so proud of me. All through school he kept on and on.

"Jimmy, I did follow his wishes. I studied diligently, and I am a good dental surgeon. But after hearing you speak today, I realize every time I look into someone's mouth I see my father's face; and so help me God, I am going to change my profession when I get home!" He turned slowly and walked away.

This was devastating—I couldn't move. Finally I leaned against the wall thinking, "What have I done? I just barely got out of high school, yet this doctor...." As strange as this may appear, I felt personally responsible for his suffering. I even thought about giving up speaking altogether.

Some time later, however, after carefully weighing it in my mind, I realized that young doctor was really *happy*. My presentation had triggered something in his memory. What he had always wanted to do from childhood had *surfaced* and become crystal-clear.

Now he would be able to mold that suppressed dream into reality.

Two years later at Sonoma State University in northern California, I learned I had been correct in reaching that conclusion. I was the banquet speaker for six-hundred-and-fifty school administrators and teachers attending a combination of break-out sessions during a full day's workshop. I sat in on all of the sessions. As a matter of fact, I arrived for breakfast. I had all day to learn as much about these individuals as I could before the banquet that night.

Here's why I was *especially* glad to be there. One session was a stress test conducted by a psychiatrist, and these were his exact words: "I must talk to any of you having a score of 150 or more on your paper because you're bordering on a heart attack or a stroke and *we need to change your department.*"

YES! Instantly my thoughts returned to that young doctor. Like him, several of these educators were unknowingly destroying themselves.

I wanted to take the test, too, and he agreed. I had never had a stress test—*never even heard of one*—however, I finished the questionnaire first.

After grading it, he looked puzzled and reported, "You have a stress of ten."

I didn't know why he had such a strange look on his face and blurted out, "That's great, isn't it, Doctor?"

"No, not really. You have to have a brain *first* before you can *have* stress!" A big, broad grin flashed across his face and we burst out laughing.

That evening I made this plea: "Following the stress test today I watched several of you discussing departmental changes with Doctor Johnson. Please don't change your department. Get out of what you're doing *altogether*. You're killing yourselves going to work every day *hating* it." I heard whispering spread throughout the room after I said that.

Please think about this. Walk into any pharmacy today and you'll find an entire wall full of assorted medications, from ulcer pills to Prozac™. This is the age of stress, nervous breakdowns, heart attacks—all because our *computers* are not doing what they really want to do! If they were, they would all cry out, "Oh, I wish I had a little more time."

Time—what a fascinating subject.

I have a sign on my office wall which reads, "When you make an appointment with another individual you accept the responsibility of punctuality and have not the right to be one minute late."

My friend, we have two things going for us on this earth and *time* is one of them. Yet, time is the one commodity over which we have no control. "Do it this way and save time" is a foolish statement we all make. You can't *save* time, you can only *spend* it. It's impossible to save one billionth of a second. Several slipped away just now while you were reading this paragraph. There is no way you can ever recover them. They are gone. Therefore, *spend* your time *wisely*. Time management is really critical.

As a reminder of how rapidly time flashes by, I love singing the catchy jingled commercial, "Pepsi Cola hits the spot, twelve full ounces that's a lot, twice as much for a nickel, too.... Pepsi Cola is the drink for you... nickel, nickel, nickel, nickel, nickel...."

It literally was the most played commercial in the history of radio.

"How long has it been since you heard that?" I often ask my audiences and hear answers ranging from twenty-five to thirty years. Let me tell you something. There hasn't been a nickel Pepsi in over forty-five years, yet we old timers remember it well.

It seems like only yesterday I was standing in front of that Methodist minister in Rush Springs, Oklahoma when he asked me, "Do you take Muriel to be your lawful wedded wife, to love....?"

I all but screamed out, "Yes sir, indeed I do. Let's get out of here!" Man, that was my wedding. I would have promised *anything!* Yes, it does seem like yesterday, but in reality, it has been more than forty-seven years. This past September 26th would have been my forty-seventh wedding anniversary. I said *would have been...* The explanation will come later. Yes, all of those memories gathered through the passage of time... locked in our *computer.*

Oh, the power of our mind. We are going to explore this matchless machine shortly and I promise you more excitement than you can anticipate.

Back to junior high school: 7th, 8th and 9th grades —young, budding adults. We shared an assembly program every Friday, and the yell leader was elected during the first one. One of my classmates from Miss Carrington's room nominated me to represent the seventh grade. I once more bounced up—this time in front of the entire student body—and surprised the others by being chosen. I was also elected the following two years and all three years in high school as well. I still hold that record. Yell leader for seven years... beginning in Miss Carrington's room that last day of grammar school.

They called me "Th' Fightin' Chick!"

When I was twelve I started delivering papers. I feel this was one of the most rewarding experiences I ever had because it was a great business lesson. I continued carrying papers until I graduated from high school.

I will never forget the day R.M. John strolled in the newspaper building talking like Donald Duck. This, to me, was absolutely the greatest thing since sliced bread, which hadn't been on the market very long either. I asked him to show me how he could imitate that voice and he did; but my attempts to copy him only resulted in irritating coughs and sputters. The other carriers disgustedly begged, "Aw, Verne, you can't do it; why don't you stop trying?"

That made me mad! I stormed back, "I'll show you I can, if it's the last thing I ever do!"

I had to learn. I spent days just trying to make the *sound*. Finally one day my hard-headed determination paid off, but then it took long months of squawks and screeches before anyone was able to understand what I said in that duck voice.

Bub and Moyne went berserk. I talked like that all of the time. I even answered the phone that way. If it was their call I would say duckishly, "Oh, it's for you," handing them the phone.

They would grab it and put their hand over the mouth piece yelling, "Mama, please don't let him answer the phone. He's crazy. He embarrasses us!" Then I would hear them speak quietly, "No, no, it's my little brother. Something is wrong with him."

Mom would console me, "Don't worry, Babe, someday we'll show them."

Once I surprised Miss Mary Bailey, my seventh grade home room teacher, with that voice. She made me stay in after school. Neither of us had the least idea that annoying duck voice would one day be the voice of a very famous television character named **Yakky Doodle** in the Yogi Bear TV series which we made in 1962, '63 and '64 and is still seen on some television cable networks today. Joe Barbera produced the series himself.

But now, forty-five years after Miss Bailey had given me that severe sermon for talking like a duck to her, I was the emcee of our 40th class reunion when she slipped up behind me and whispered, "Do you remember when I made you stay in after school for answering me like that duck?" I smiled, nodding yes.

"I was always afraid I might have inhibited you," she apologized.

I laughed out loud. "Yes, Miss Bailey, you really hurt me!" I don't have to tell you, she was my all-time favorite *feminine-gendered* teacher and I look forward to seeing her today at every one of our reunions —now fifty-eight years later.

Jimmy Wakely traveled throughout Oklahoma holding amateur contests at movie theatres. The winner's prize was a guest appearance on his radio show in Oklahoma City. I entered one singing "Three Little Fishes" like Donald Duck.

Here is that wonderful teacher whom I love so much ... Miss Mary Bailey. She showed such dedication to her students she was given a special award by the reunion class in 1994 which read:

Teacher of the Twentieth Century

Jimmy held his hand over each contestant's head and the winner was determined by the loudest applause. I was mortified when he got to me, because boos rang throughout the theatre. I ran off of the stage crying. I had never suffered such humiliation. I was finished with show business.

Trying my best to go out the back door, Jimmy grabbed me. "Laverne, I've never heard anyone imitate Donald Duck as good as you can."

"I'm never going to do it again, either."

He shook my arms. "Listen, don't you want to be in show business?"

"Yes sir, I thought I did, but... I'm not... sure now."

Still squeezing my arms firmly, he demanded, "Laverne, I want you to go home and write an act of Donald Duck and his three nephews. Memorize it and give it on this stage the next time I'm here."

I shook my head, but he persisted, "Promise me you'll be here!" I agreed and left, almost afraid to tell Mom and the others after I got home what had taken place. You see, my entry into the contest had been *my own idea.* Finally, I did confess my embarrassment and Bub and Moyne were overjoyed because I'd failed so miserably. They mumbled, "Now maybe he'll stop being so silly."

Mom, bless her heart, once more came to my mental rescue. "Babe, don't worry, I'll help you write an act and it will be great."

"Mama, you mean it?" I begged.

"Yes, I do," and she hugged me.

Together we wrote an act of "Donald Duck and His Three Nephews Going To The Rodeo."

Three or four weeks later, Jimmy Wakely returned

to the Rialto Theatre, where five years earlier I had seen my first movie—the guide to my future. This time I was the winner.

Nothing would stop me now!!!

Approximately 55 years later ...

Yep, the old man is *me*—as a preacher, performing a double wedding ceremony on the sitcom, *It's A Living*. Little Webster never changes. He stays the same—three years old... hmmmm. Oh well... by the way, the whiskers are real. *Weldon, you are old.*

3. King, Queen & Three Jacks

I wish everyone could experience the sincere love I had as a little guy.

Dad...was the head of our family. No one ever questioned his authority, yet he was as gentle as a lamb. He weighed 150 pounds and his eyes were sort of greenish-brown, dancing with a sparkle.

Dad was five-feet-seven-and-one-half inches tall, but when he was about to give me a spanking, which I certainly deserved, he looked more like a giant to me. I don't think he attended school after the third grade, but he was an Einstein in math... and his real talent was psychology.

I didn't like doing my home work which had to be turned in the next day at school. Today some youngsters have an attention span deficit. Sixty years ago, some called it *"you-are-just-not-interested"*— which reminds me of a fella who made the statement, "When I was growing up, our family was so poor we couldn't even pay attention."

Dad knew how to solve my whatever-it-was by simply insisting that I "read the problem and *think* about what was being asked." That reminder was enough to keep me on track.

He helped Bub and Moyne in high school with their math and his calculations were always right, but he couldn't tell how he came up with the answers. He really didn't know.

D ad was *genuinely* funny. He owned a Texaco service station and loved serving his customers.

If anyone asked him how he was feeling, they always heard the same reply, "If I felt any better, I couldn't stand it!" I copied Dad and have used those same words for sixty-plus years.

Most of his hair disappeared early in life; just a little around the back of his head to his ears was all there was. He wore his Texaco cap faithfully, but when he took it off he made this silly confession, "I wear this to keep the hair out of my eyes." Naturally people laughed when they saw his baldness. Then he rubbed his head, comparing it to a smooth used tire, and announced, "This isn't age—it's mileage."

His favorite expression describing someone really smiling from ear to ear, so to speak, was: "He was grinning *like a cat eating glue.*"

I n 1955, I tore the end of my finger completely off in a ridiculous lawn mower accident and another favorite expression of Dad's came to mind immediately: "Experience is the one thing a guy gets just after he no longer needs it." Oh, how true.

That was almost forty-years ago, and *I promise most assuredly I am never going to stick my hand in a belt and pulley again.* By the way, this accident happened in my back yard. I couldn't faint, because I was alone. There was no audience.

D ad possessed a photographic memory. He memorized addresses, telephone numbers, and credit cards ... you-name-it. Everything.

One day a car drove into the station and he greeted this couple as usual, "Good morning, neighbors. May I help you, please?"

"Yes. Fill it up."

"Fine. Thank you, sir."

Dad really did own a *service* station. He checked the tires, oil, washed the windshield.... He even swept the floor out with a little broom.

The gasoline was filling the tank automatically while Dad was doing those things, but he was upset because he couldn't remember the man's name. He finally walked to the driver's window and apologized.

"I'm sorry I can't recall your name, sir."

Dad's innocent remark annoyed the man.

He probably thought: this poor fool's trying to use psychology to make me feel at home.

"No wonder," he snarled, "I've never been in this damn place before."

Dad wasn't expecting such an answer. "Well, I guess you reminded me of someone else."

"Yeah," again the man snapped sarcastically.

Then it *hit* him. Keeping his big grin, Dad cleverly added another apology. "Sir, you are right. I don't know you. But *had* you been the man I first thought you were, I would have asked about your green Chevrolet and that little dog that I liked so much."

The man was beside himself. "My, God. He ... he... he... knows... me!" he sputtered to his wife. Then turning back to Dad, he said, "I don't even know what town this is and I haven't had that green Chevrolet in two years."

Nuf sed!

Here's my Dad again—as I saw him during my school years—
in his Texaco uniform. Yes, this is a very old photograph...
made with a box camera, in about 1932. The spot on Dad's
left cheek is a film error... as are the other speckles, too.

We boys appreciated Mom and Dad's total unselfish commitment to us and felt we owed them so much, but Dad's philosophy was rare. "You boys owe us nothing. We owe *you* everything. You are uninvited guests into this world. You didn't ask to be born—we asked for you. Anything you do is a reflection on Mom and me. When you do something good, we can hold our heads up proudly and say, 'Those are our boys,' but if you do something ugly, we have to bow our heads and ask for forgiveness, because we didn't teach you right."

With a Dad like that, how can a guy go wrong?

He referred to our family as:

"The King... Queen... and Three Jacks."

Mom... the Queen. Ah, yes. Mom was about five-feet-five-inches tall. She had soft, brown eyes and her hair was rich, thick and black as the ace of spades. Here is the way she described her weight. "I weighed ninety-eight pounds when your father and I were married." When friends came by and we started talking about the good ol' days, she would go to a drawer and bring out a few old, grainy photographs and sure enough, there she was at the ninety-eight pound limit. However, *my* idea of motherhood was a wonderful, beautiful lady always standing on bathroom scales—dieting and drifting between 150 and 175 pounds—who loved her family very, very much. 'Specially *me*.

Leaving the physical appearances now, I was the baby, so Mom was my real buddy. She was always home. She and Dad did without everything unless it was an absolute necessity. We boys were their lives.

Yes, Mom *did* have that slender build when they were wed. Here's a genuine 1917-model marriage... which truly lasted a lifetime.

Ooooops... Mom sampled too much of that good food she cooked for Dad, Bub, Moyne and me. The 98 pounds... uh... but she was beautiful!

No one ever had a Mom and Dad they could say they loved more than Bub, Moyne and me.

Bub... my big brother, almost six feet tall in the 7th grade. He was the fullback all through junior and high school. He was also the best high jumper, shot putt thrower, javelin thrower, discus thrower, hurdler... whatever. Bubba's name was engraved on most of the trophies in the big display case in the hallway at high school.

BIG JOE SHINN WINS AGAIN

Those were the headlines prominent in the Daily Express and I was delivering them to my customers.

Yahooooooo! My brother!

But there is more. What a baseball player! Bubba's first gifts were a ball and glove. Yes, when he was two years old Dad used to throw him a ball. He was hardly walking! You see, Dad's greatest desire was to have a son playing professional baseball. Dad knew every player on major league teams, their batting averages... everything!

After Bub graduated from high school he went to a camp for young baseball players sponsored by the Saint Louis Cardinals. Mr. Branch Ricky, one of the all time great coaches and managers, was present. He recognized Bub's outstanding ability almost immediately and asked him his age. His answer surprised Mr. Ricky.

"Seventeen, sir."

"Son, you don't have to lie to me."

"Mr. Ricky, I *am* seventeen, sir."

Shaking his head he confessed softly, "I have never seen a baseball player with the talent you have at

I told you Bub was big. Moyne and I are sitting on his arms... Wow! Bub's in junior high school.

this age, Joe."

He came to our house with a contract for Bub and Daddy was so thrilled we almost had to peel him off of the ceiling. At long last, his dream was coming true, but Mom had been taught as a child that it was a *sin* to play baseball on Sunday. She could not erase that thought from her *computer*.

Yes, dear reader, that happened more than fifty-eight years ago. Our attitudes have changed regarding many things since then, but Bub would never do anything Mom thought was wrong. Had he accepted that opportunity, I believe the Baseball Hall of Fame would proudly include his name today.

Later in life, Mom wanted so badly to believe she hadn't actually used her influence in his decision not to play. *Influence?* That was the *only* reason he didn't play!

Bub is now retired and has often admitted, "I never enjoyed a single day of my life at work *on any job I ever had.*"

I will always feel like Bub's life and that young doctor in the last chapter parallel one another, yet are almost exact opposites. Bub was not a professional baseball player because of Mom. The dental surgeon was a surgeon because of his Dad. Both were parents showing a deep love for their sons, but what a difference in the way it was *innocently administisistered*.

Re-examine the title of this book.

I *fully understand* Bub's feelings. He never did what he really wanted to do. Bless his heart, he isn't alone. Only one in twenty ever does. Fortunately, I am one of them.

M oyne... the middle brother... the handsome one. Moyne was a good baseball and basketball player like Bub, too.

Bub and I constantly yelled, while Moyne sat quietly, sadly shaking his head. When he *did* talk we all listened because he had something to say.

In high school he wrote the following verse in honor of Mom's father, whom we called Papa—a wonderful grandfather who lived to the ripe old age of a few months less than one hundred years.

There often live where mortals trod
Men of greatness, unacclaimed;
By whose choice in silence dwell,
Unknown... but to God.

A well deserved tribute to Papa.

Moyne has proven so many times the truth in one of his pet phrases: "There is no corner on brains!"

Well, there we were. As I drop in various incidents, you will visualize these individuals who have played the true roles in my life.

4. Hollywood Comes to Chickasha

One of my happiest memories—being a celebrity guest in 1980 for a charity golf tournament at Hilton Head Island, South Carolina. I visited for more than an hour with a *real* celebrity, the late Spanky McFarland, of Our Gang comedies. He was as down-to-earth as anyone you would ever want to meet. In my opinion, this was such a rare opportunity because Our Gang comedies have been seen around the world for more than sixty years. We all change as Father Time passes, so he wasn't that chubby little guy with the round face, now he was an old chubby little guy with a round face. My point is, if anyone had heard, "Look! Spanky McFarland is sitting over there," more than ninety per cent would have said excitedly, "Where?"—rather than "Who?"—if television were available in their area.

Please return with me more than 59 years ago when I was eleven. Mom read in the paper a Hollywood company was scheduling a trip to small towns throughout America making Our Gang comedy films. The talent would be children living in each town and the films would be shown in one of the local theatres. The actors *paid* to be in the movie. Mom saw Chickasha on the list and we made plans for my first movie. You talk about plans—we had 'em.

Audition day! Everybody was there for try-outs. Mom and I felt like we knew who would get the big part. Dear friend, there is a huge difference between *confidence* and *smart aleckness*. I had known for four years I was going to be an actor someday. I was no little kid with his mother pushing him into show business. We were prepared! The seed, planted when I was 7, had germinated and was popping up out of the ground.

When my name was called to read for a part, I listened intently to Mr. Barker, the director, and I was chosen as the *star*. Mom was so thrilled. Me, too! Where were Bub and Moyne? At home. Actors? No way. That was dumb!

The next two weeks after school and on weekends were filled with making a movie. Mothers and children caravaned all over Chickasha. It was the greatest. I ate up every word, absorbing anything to do with movie making. The time flashed by, ending everything so quickly, but the day to see the completed film finally came and the theatre never ever had as many people waiting. Bub and Moyne were a bit excited, too.

When the title appeared, I all but jumped out of my seat. Then seeing myself, I nearly died. My heart was pounding so hard. Of course everyone felt this way. No, not really. I had dreamed of being there more than anyone. Golleeeee! *I can still remember that feeling,* which was repeated twelve years later at the Royal Academy Of Dramatic Arts in London, England. One of our instructors made these comments: "There are three categories of the theatre. One is true genius—that being the person who writes, directs and stars in a play, such as Noel Coward. Next is the director who interprets the author's writing and gives the actors proper directions. Last is the actor. Anyone who can take directions is a good craftsman, and Jimmy Weldon is the one person in this class who can follow directions." At that moment I was as proud as that little boy with his family seeing himself for the first time on the screen in Chickasha.

Did all of my performances end happily? I'm afraid not. Mom was a terrific piano and organ player. We always had a piano in our house. Bub decided I should sing a solo for his Sunday school class. Me? Certainly. Why not? I can sing and my partner, Mom, will accompany me. We rehearsed day-in and day-out till Bub was almost ready to cancel it, but that day did arrive. Oh, by the way, the hymn I was to sing is Open Mine Eyes. I had no idea how much it would open mine or I never would have chosen it, or *any other* for that matter. I never would have *been* the soloist.

The teacher announced, "Laverne, Joe Weldon's little brother, is going to sing Open Mine Eyes and their mother, Mrs. Shinn, will accompany him."

I stood up and nodded to Mom, as if to say, "Let 'er go, Mom. I'm ready!"

She played the introduction and I started belting out the song, looking down at the hymnal. Near the end of the chorus following the first verse, I glanced up. The whole class (at least ten counting Mom and me) was quietly sitting there. I thought, "What in the world am I doing?" and swallowed a lump as big as a mule. Yes, I was choking. Mom's mouth was wide open in disbelief. I could hear people breathing. I felt little beads of perspiration forming around my nose, yet it wasn't even warm. How I made it through the next two verses will always remain a mystery. I remembered how much fun it had been making the movie. How on earth did I let myself get into this awful mess? Dad-gum!

The mind is a strange thing. That memory still lingers and though it was just a childhood moment of uncertainty, doubt, lack of confidence, it was indelibly planted in that vast resource of untapped energy—*my mind*—and I never got it out. I could have, had I honestly tried and sincerely wanted to, but no, it never was *that* important. Oh, I sang in the church choir, in the glee club at school and on television with little Webster as comedy, but never *alone*.

How easily I can sense when someone has no confidence and finds it frightening to even make a little announcement before a group. I wonder if maybe they experienced miserable failure, perhaps in a speech class, and they keep reliving that failure over and over again every day; when in reality, it should have merely been a learning step, *not the end result.*

I'm one of the most fortunate entertainers God has ever let live. I have spoken to more National Management Association chapters now than any speaker in the United States: Ford Motor Co., TRW, Bendix, General Dynamics, Rockwell, GTE, AT&T, Lockheed, McDonnell-Douglas, and Hughes, to name a few.

I may ask the program chairman, "How much time do I have to speak?"

If I am told, "You have 30 minutes," my reply is always, "I *bow* that long!"

Just don't ask me to sing a solo.

5. "Shoot them first... let *me* be last!"

For several years, my good friend, Charles Runnels, Chancellor of Pepperdine University, has honored me with the distinction of serving as the banquet speaker for the Southern California Youth Citizenship Seminar. I am especially grateful because the parents are also present.

Each year, two-hundred-and-fifty top scholars spend a week on this beautiful campus while industry executives introduce them to our American free enterprise system.

Goal setting and motivation to achieve them should be an essential segment in our schools' curriculum. It's a shame only one person in twenty is motivated. Young people aren't shown real leadership, they're just taught what *not* to do. Don't do this! Don't do that!

Think about it. We all started life the same way. The first nine months were spent on a water bed. Mom fed us and kept us warm and comfortable, but when we made our entrance into the world the doctor held us upside down and spanked us. What a horrible way to start life, but you did. Frankly that's not true; not everybody did. I was so ugly the doctor slapped my mother instead of me. She took one look and said, "I'll never let him breast feed, I would just rather have him as a friend." Uh, not really.

But then all of us suffered the unpardonable sin—

the severing of our umbilical cord. At this point, we were completely alone for the first time.

Imagine seeing one hundred little babies lying in cribs, side by side, as doctors separate their umbilical cords. From that moment, ninety-five of those little fellas will start looking for another place to plug it back in—for security. No, that's no joke. Many of them will spend the rest of their lives looking for that *plug*.

I mentioned how children are taught negatively in school, but what about our lessons at home—the formative years—our most impressionable period?

Don't love too deeply, you might get hurt.

Don't speak unless you are spoken to.

Don't go where you are not wanted.

Don't step in *that!*

Well, if you happen to be from Texas or Oklahoma, you'll understand that last one, for sure. We are all conditioned.

D id you know scientists place little fleas on a table, then cover them with a clear bowl?

It's an experiment to show how they can be conditioned to jump in the air much lower than they normally do. Here's how it works. These little fleas don't realize there is a bowl over their heads and they have strong legs. When they decide to jump, wham!— they hit their heads on this bowl. They can't see it and wonder what in the world they are smashing into. You must remember now, we're talking about fleas—just ordinary ol' dog fleas. Well, after only a few leaps smashing their heads, even tiny fleas have enough sense to think, "Dad-gum, this is dumb! If we don't jump quite as high as we are now we won't hit our heads," so they start taking little hops about one-quarter-of-an-inch high. When the scientists see the fleas bouncing at this lower level, they remove the bowl and *these little fellas will never jump any higher.* They're conditioned to a new jumping height.

You're probably saying, who cares? Well, here's another one. You'll find aquariums in the reception areas of doctors' offices more often than any other buildings. Patients somehow don't appear as nervous while watching fish swim in a labyrinth of little castles and rock formations in these watery shows.

Doctors, bless their hearts, must possess a very special talent indeed, choosing a profession where 99% of their clients are suffering some kind of misery. This is evident because all they hear every day, from the first patient till the last, is "Oh, doctor, help me. Help me, please." Patients can only tell the doctor how they feel and they wouldn't be there if they felt *good.* Whoever heard of an individual running into a doctor's office yelling, "Man, do I feel great. I made this appointment with you today just to tell you how good I feel. Yahooo! How much do I owe you?" No sir, that's dumb! I wouldn't trade places with a doctor if he or she made ten thousand dollars a minute. I mean that. Well, I might work a couple of days, but *then* I'd quit!

The atmosphere in the reception room is one of complete silence. You never know but what the person next to you may be dying of cancer. You don't want to scream out what a beautiful day it is, or at least you don't *think you should*, so you don't. Perhaps now you can see why so many aquariums are found in these areas.

A rectangular aquarium was the arena for an incredible experiment. Scientists placed a thin sheet of clear plexiglass down the center, dividing it in two halves. A small Spanish mackerel was dropped in one side and in the other, a barracuda, a little fish that looks like all teeth and mouth. Spanish mackerel is his favorite food. When he saw this mackerel, he rammed his head into the glass to reach him. He couldn't see the glass, so he had no idea what was stopping him. He backed off and came racing toward the mackerel again. Wham! Crashing into this invisible barrier, he kept repeating this over and over.

On the opposite side was the Spanish mackerel watching—as far away as possible—but thinking, "I don't know why he isn't over here, but I'm glad he can't make it."

Well, it didn't take too many bashes of his nose to let the barracuda (like the fleas) figure out *this is dumb* and stop trying to get to his *food*. When the scientists were convinced the barracuda had given up, they removed the glass partition and in time, the two fish swam to the center of the aquarium, but neither would pass it. The mackerel knew he would remain safe on his side and the barracuda didn't want to bash his nose again—on something that was no longer there. Can you hear me?

Moving right along now, you've seen a giant elephant by a circus tent with a little rope holding one leg. When that big old pachyderm was a baby, the trainer chained that leg to a piece of steel firmly anchored in twelve feet of concrete. The elephant pulled and tugged, often causing his little leg to fester and bleed. This was not punishment, the trainer was only conditioning him to stand in one place, whenever he was chained by *that* leg. In time, he stopped trying to get free.

Fifty years later, that *same* leg is tied with a rope to a stake driven less than eighteen inches in the ground. This elephant won't even attempt to move because he doesn't *think* he can and he also remembers how much it hurt when he did try to move.

The first law of nature is self-preservation. I don't care whether it's a flea, a fish, an elephant or whatever. This is for *anything* that is alive. There have been circus fires causing people to scream and run in panic... complete bedlam... yet this big ol' elephant will remain still. Before he dies from smoke inhalation or burns, he musters enough courage to try once more to free himself.

When he moves, it really angers him because he doesn't even *feel* the rope. He suddenly understands, "Those jerks had me tied down for fifty years!" and you'll never restrain him in that manner again. You can chain him to a building and he'll pull the building and all over. It only took that one incident for him to realize he had been conditioned all those years to stand *wherever* he was chained.

Perhaps you're thinking, "Jimmy, this is ridiculous. I'm no flea, fish or elephant." That's true, but if you know anything about the game of golf, you will appreciate audiences laughing as I describe the way most of us golfers *think* when standing on a tee, looking out across one hundred yards of water to a little postage stamp green.

Our *computers* automatically whisper, "Maybe you had better tee up one of your water balls to hit over that pond." Through conditioning, we're afraid of losing another *good* one to the resident fish. That strikes a familiar chord to you golfers, doesn't it?

One more truth about self preservation. Say you were in a room with a hundred others when three men holding machine guns rushed in demanding that everybody line up against the wall. If one of the group should ask, "Why do you want us to stand up against the wall?" and the simple reply was, "Because we're going to kill everyone in this room," I seriously doubt if you would rush forward and shout, "Oh I'm so happy. I've been waiting for you. Come on in!"

No, I rather believe you might scream, "Wait! Wait! Shoot *them* first... let *me* be last!" It's a strange thing. Everybody wants to go to heaven, but nobody wants to die to get there. 'Nuf sed!

I tell students you're hurting someone rather than helping them any time you do something *for* them they should do for themselves. I explain how scientists place a little mouse in a bowl of warm water. The little fella can't walk on the bottom because the water's too deep. He can't crawl out over the top because the lip's too high, so he swims until his body can't move any more and he sinks, drowning. They lift him out of the bowl, clear the water from his lungs, feed him, let him rest—and then put him back in the bowl. I hear "ohhh" and "awww" from the students, because they feel sorry for this little rodent. I remind them the mouse has drowned once, and ask how long they think he'll swim this time. Half as long, as long, or twice as long?"

"*Twice* as long!" is the usual loud response. They're shocked to hear he'll swim slightly more than half as long because he thinks, "They rescued me before, so as soon as I quit swimming they'll get me out of here again." And that's a little mouse. What about... a *human*?"

Furthermore, students are surprised at the results of a third generation welfare recipient's interview. Two men visited a seventeen year old young man who had never seen his father or grandfather with employment of any nature. They asked him if there was anything he wanted and he shook his head. No, he was happy with his life just as it was. Soon he realized their visit was not to criticize him for being lazy, they really *wanted* to help him if they could.

He finally confessed quietly, "Well, there *was* a car I saw once I'd like to have." That simple, honest statement gave the men something to really zero in on. They asked him to describe that car and he did. Every tiny detail.

"Come with us."

"Where?"

"You're going to learn how to drive that car."

"I'm what?"

"You're going to drive that car yourself."

When they arrived at the dealership the young man pointed, "That's the car! There!"

While he was learning to drive that car, they snapped pictures of him at different locations. His instructions continued until he was skilled enough to take the driver's test. He passed it!

Here was the most important part of all. They handed him those pictures saying they were his special reward for passing the exam. He thanked them, promising to show his father and grandfather, but the real help depended on his following their next request. "Hang these photographs up on the walls all through your house, son, and *look* at them."

He did. Each day he strolled through his home looking at those pictures. They were not out of some magazine, they were pictures of him. He was driving that car. He had the license to prove he could drive. He became more and more excited and in less than three weeks, he got a job. You see, this was the first time he'd ever been motivated to do *anything*.

If you don't believe this is real stimulation, have your picture taken with something *you* want. Make several copies and do exactly as that young man. Scatter them through your house. I promise, you'll wind up with the same results. You can't believe what those pictures will do to you, or rather, *for* you. Whatever you see and weave a desire for is something you'll *struggle to acquire!*

P lanting a goal in one's mind is the most important decision an individual can make.

Our *computer* will accomplish whatever it's asked to do. We are all guided by our thoughts. Think back. There's nothing you have ever done that you didn't first *think* you could do, but your *desire* to do it was equally as important.

I love the example of a ship anchored in the harbor with the captain and crew on board. When it leaves the dock, the ship might travel weeks on open seas and never see dry land, but the crew knows where it's going. You can rest assured it will arrive because it has a definite *goal*.

Let that same ship leave with no captain or crew on board. You have to realize immediately there's no way it can go anywhere with no guidance system and no destination. It will ram into something and sink.

Imagine the results of a house built with no plans. The workmen would be stumbling all over each other. Building materials would be scattered here and there and even before the foundation was laid, they would start putting up the walls. Everybody on the job would have a different idea how it should be built. What would happen? Confusion, anger, misunderstandings—and you can forget the expense. There's *no way* it could be finished.

Next... by using a small magnifying glass you can see the importance of having a definite goal. Focus the sunrays on a specific spot of wood and you'll quickly see a little curl of smoke because it will burn a hole very fast. Move the magnifying glass away from the wood (which represents a definite goal) and the rays of the sun could shine on that same spot for a million years and never burn it. Okay?

"Place all your eggs in one basket and then watch the basket to see that no one kicks it over." Those are the words Andrew Carnegie advised his colleagues to do. I *love* it.

I've asked college students to define their plans after graduation and you'd be alarmed at how many have no idea what they're going to do. I had one fellow yell out, "I don't care what I do when I graduate. I just want to make a lot of money."

I yelled right back, "If that's what you want to do, go work in a mint, because the only people who make money work in a mint."

I then heard a soft reply, "I didn't mean that." Of course he didn't mean *that*, but that's exactly what he was telling his *computer*... absolutely nothing! You have to know *precisely* what it is you want.

Until Fotomat began operations, bad negatives were thrown away. I mention that only to remind you that any goal you may have which is not completely spelled out will end up like a bad negative. In all probability, you won't finish but about half of it without some definite guidelines.

There is one thing you can do better than anyone else in the world. Search your heart and *computer* to find this particular *thing* and then make it your concrete goal. In your search, you'll discover what it is you would like to do best. That 'whatever - it-is' will be the one thing you will immerse *your whole heart and soul* into for its accomplishment.

Motivation and goal setting are synonymous. The person who says *I can* and one who says *I cannot* are both right one hundred per cent of the time.

There are three individuals in each of us: the Jimmy Weldon I *am*, the one I want you to *think* I am, and the Jimmy Weldon *I want to be*. Number three is the most meaningful by far.

Becoming the person you want to be and doing what you really want to do is the secret of success. Here is a poem that expresses it so beautifully.

If you think you are beaten, you are;
If you think you dare not, you don't;
If you like to win, but you think you can't,
It is almost certain you won't.
If you think you'll lose, you've lost,
For out of the world we find
Success begins with a fellow's will;
It's all in the state of mind.

If you think you are outclassed, you are;
You've got to think high to rise.
You've got to be sure of yourself
Before you can ever win a prize.

Life's battles don't always go
To the stronger or faster man;
But soon or late the man who wins
Is the man who thinks he can.

Now, continuing the journey, here is my reason for including the last several examples. Benjamin Bernard Barr was also a paper boy. We became inseparable companions and talked about our dreams constantly. We agreed that my future in Hollywood would produce a great deal of money, and he was to be my accountant. Yes, as young boys, Bennie and I felt the sky truly *was* the limit.

"Bennie, get the knowledge necessary."

"I will, Verne."

In show business we say, "Fade to black and come up on a new scene."

This is Bennie, my very best friend in junior and senior high school. Let's say this was taken in about 1938 or 1939, huh?

Our childhood fantasies began about 1936. Forty years later, during our second high school class reunion (1976), each one was relating the things they had done after graduation. I was sitting beside Bennie and his wife, Dorotha, when my turn came. I explained our being a team; how I'd earn the money and Bennie would take care of it. I laughed. I'd been out here since 1952 and never earned enough money to *require* attention.

Bennie stood up and smiled, "I did *my* part. What Laverne and I talked about. I got my degree and was a partner in a nationwide accounting firm."

Bennie also wrote a college text book on accounting. You talk about doing his part. *Wow!*

After many years, Bennie dissolved his accounting partnership and was now helping others with their spiritual goals. Yes, Bennie was a minister, for which I am so thankful.

I merely wanted to emphasize how the 'planted seeds' of two young boys sharing their special dreams had matured. Indeed they had. For Bennie.

My misunderstanding of the *money* part of our dreams will be explained in a later chapter.

6. Actions *do* speak louder than words!

One of the subjects Bub and Moyne took in high school was typing. Dad bought a typewriter for them to practice at home. The keys were covered, which made it necessary to memorize the location of each letter. I'd stand behind them and found it so intriguing I begged them to teach me. Well, between the two, I mastered this unusual skill and could hardly wait to take typing in high school.

Can you imagine the look on my teacher's face during our first exam? Everyone slowly pecking away at the speed of about five words a minute while I was leisurely grinning *like Dad's cat* and pounding out more than thirty. My typewriter sounded like a jack hammer by comparison.

As a gentle reminder, Bub is almost five years older than I am, so he was the first family typist. And then came Moyne. I had four years of actual experience before ever receiving any legitimate tutoring. My report card glowed with straight A's. I had a ball!

In the last several years, I've enjoyed speaking to more and more school administrators and teachers. Bless their hearts, teachers are the most important segment of our society. Their guidance is the key to our young people's future. One action can change a student's life.

Case in point: In the eleventh grade, I decided to take algebra. I never was good at math but I felt it was a subject I needed.

My teacher was Mr. Claude Welch. On the first day, while explaining what we could expect from his class, he turned to write something on the blackboard when I called out, "Mr. Welch, what does....?" Writing this today, I don't have the slightest idea what my question was, but I'm sure I thought it was really important *then*, however his answer rendered whatever it was meaningless.

He paused, turned around looking directly at me for what seemed an eternity, lifted his hand to his mouth slowly, pulling his fingers down under his chin. You could have heard a pin drop. The absolute silence in the room was deafening. Finally he gradually turned back and began writing.

You talk about humiliation! Four years earlier when they booed me off of the stage was *applause* by comparison. I was shattered beyond all recovery! My mind raced! Mr. Welch, you made a mistake, sir, by not answering me.

The instant the bell rang I hurried to the Superintendent's office, explaining what had happened and declared I was never going back. I begged him to assign me another subject. *Any* subject! He tried to dissuade me, but I was determined.

Following algebra was study hall, the last class of the day, so I went home. It wasn't long before Mr. Holesapple summoned me to his office.

"Laverne, you've been missing your algebra class."

"Yes, sir. I told you, Mr. Holesapple, I wasn't going back to Mr. Welch."

"Where have you been? You've missed study hall as well?"

"I go home right after English class. There's no reason to walk around here for an hour, then go to study hall."

"Oh, you say you've been going straight home?" He looked at me skeptically.

That really hurt. I stretched across his desk and grabbed the phone, dialed our house and passed it to him *before* it even began ringing. I knew Mom would be there. She was.

"Mrs. Shinn, I didn't want to bother you. Laverne called and handed me the telephone. He said he has been going home every afternoon after, uh...." Mom cut him off to explain exactly what he was about to ask her.

"Yes, that's what he said, uh. I will. Thank you, Mrs. Shinn," and hung up.

Now smiling, "All right, Laverne, what do you want to take?" I took two six-month courses so I could graduate with my class the following year.

I never spoke to Mr. Welch again. I confess harboring feelings of resentment 41 years. All those years—until our 1981 reunion. As emcee, I knew many of our teachers would be present. I could hardly wait to stand at the podium and point to Mr. Welch, "Now that I'm up here and you're sitting out there, Mr. Welch, I want to tell you something. You literally destroyed me the first day of algebra in 1940 when you....!" This was really going to be my big moment!

Just before our banquet, I was visiting in the home of another dear friend and classmate, Seabrook Griffin and his wife, Billie Jean. I enthusiastically shared my satisfaction at figuring out such a clever way to *get even* with Mr. Welch after all those years. I practiced in front of them what I'd planned to do, confident it would go over *big* with Seabrook, but I was certainly wrong. A sad expression replaced his smile. (He's one of the few who called me 'Jimmy' after I returned from the war.)

He quietly admonished, "Jimmy, you can't do that."

"*What?*" I blurted out boldly.

Still quietly, "He has had a couple of strokes and is very ill. He has no idea he hurt you and you might make him wonder how many other students feel the same way but never told him."

As I listened, my mind initiated a complete turn. I wanted to hug Seabrook. All of my hatred, 41 years, melted, and I suddenly found I wanted to apologize to Mr. Welch for something of which he wasn't even *aware.*

I said nothing at the banquet, but to those of you who may be teachers or contemplating becoming one, please think carefully before every behavior or comment to your students. A single action or word can have lasting effect on their lives.

Remember, this happened in *1981!*

While re-reading this chapter a few minutes ago, I began crying. I dialed Mr. Welch's number in Chickasha and recorded the following conversation:

"Hello," the lady answered.

"Mrs. Welch?"

"Yes?"

"Is your husband, Mr. Claude Welch, there?"

"Yes."

"May I speak to him, please?"

"He is in a rest home, sir."

"Oh. Then I can't talk to him. Would you please give him a message for me?"

"Yes, I will be glad to."

"I know this name won't mean a thing to you, but my name is Jimmy Weldon... and... it is really Laverne Shinn... it used to be that before...."

"Th' fightin' chick!" she quickly broke in.

"I beg your pardon?"

"Th' fightin' chick!" she repeated. And this time I understood.

"Yes, darling, I am th' fightin' chick!"

"Yes, I knew that," and I felt a big smile in her voice.

"I'm crying now, but I don't mean to. I'm writing a book, Mrs. Welch."

"You are?"

"Yes, Ma'am, and I was just writing about a little incident that happened in his algebra class and I wanted to tell him that I love him. Tell him I love him. Will you please?"

"I wish you could go and see him," she said quietly.

"I do, too. Where is he?"

"He's here in Chickasha at the, uh, rest home on 9th street. I can't remember the name of it."

"Is he all right?"

"His mind is not very good. He has had two very serious strokes."

"Oh, golly! I just wish I could tell him that!"

"Well, I will tell him for you."

"Please do. Please tell him."

"I will, and he will appreciate that... and I appreciate your thinking of him."

"Thank you, Mrs. Welch. Bye bye."

Maybe, just maybe, this will mean something to him. In all likelihood, he forgot all about it shortly after it happened. I mean waaaay back in 1940! *But I had never forgotten.* Even though I had removed it from my *computer* with Seabrook and Billie Jean just before the banquet in 1981, I still felt more at peace just now following my conversation with Mrs. Welch. I am sure she has no idea why I begged her to be sure and give Mr. Welch that message. Only I had held it... so deeply. The present? 1990.

And Seabrook, if this book is ever finished and published, I want you to know...

I love you, too, ol' friend!

Small P.S.
This is the second printing and some changes have been updated in my book. Mr. Welch has since passed away, but this report of the algebra class incident still holds more *impossible-to-fully-relate-from-the-heart* meaning to me than any other section. It's now January of 1995.

7. The Supreme Powerhouse

We are living in the age of computers. New concepts in electronics are now developing more rapidly than industry can manufacture consumer products.

Computers can accomplish things man will never duplicate. For example, we have four registers. One contains the names of all automobile owners in America; another, the home owners; number three lists taxpayers and the fourth one... all veterans.

We give them to a computer and a clerk asking each to make a list with names found on all *four* lists. Next, we ask for a list naming veterans, home and automobile owners but leave off the taxpayers. Then, we want a single list of taxpayers and veterans but omit the car and home owners.

A computer could print them quicker than a burst from a machine gun, yet it would require *months* for the clerk to do so.

Check this: We have a computer programmed to play chess. It has the capability of calculating its opponent's potential moves at the rate of one million per second.

But hold on, there happens to be a silent running dynamo of creativity, memory and reason which makes that chess playing machine look like a tricycle next to an Indianapolis speed racer. This *computer* runs on power sources ranging from rice to roast beef. More than five billion are in use and will run for decades without any repairs *if* taken care of properly. Each weighs about three pounds, is 85% water and has the consistency of jelly, needing the skull to hold its shape. Yes, dear friend, when it comes to intellectual vigor, nothing can equal your *brain*.

Speaking to students, I'll lift up a glass of water and pretend it's pure alcohol. Gulping down a few swallows I gag, spew, sputter, cough and look wide-eyed. After a second or two I grab my stomach in terrible pain. After straightening up, I place my finger next to my temple explaining, "Our *computer* is like the leader of a wolf pack. It eats before any other organ in our body. Now, if this glass *had* been filled with alcohol, my *computer* wouldn't know it was a dangerous substance and would demand it first!

"Young people, every minute one-and-a-half pints of blood flow through your brain carrying the four hundred calories it needs to generate the 25 watts of power on which it runs. It also carries *whatever else* is in it. I said every minute, 24 hours a day, seven days a week. What you place *in* that blood is of your own choice."

Why don't you take a break now and look in the mirror. Examine the face of the only person you're never going to leave... **yourself!**

The human brain contains perhaps one hundred billion neurons. These tiny nerve cells receive and transmit thousands of signals simultaneously and each one is connected to thousands of others. One expert states that a cubic millimeter of brain cortex probably has ten trillion neural links, making the total memory connections infinite.

Everything you do, every thought you think, everything you see, every nod of your head, every bat of your eyes was first chemistry and electricity rushing through the neurons in your brain. We do hundreds of thousands of things each day from putting on our shoes to passing the salt and pepper and each of those actions is stored in our brain. No, we don't carry them *up front* for instant recall, but they're there.

E veryone has experienced déjà vu. These are times when you suddenly think to yourself, "Oh, golly, I've done this before. I know I have. I know what's going to take place next. Yeah, yeah, I know exactly what, uh, golly... maybe it happened in another life."

Please listen, dear friend. Those actions you relive *were* experienced many, many other times, but you were not conscious of them then because you were *focusing* on something else.

Did you ever stop and wonder why your back was itching, or your eye had a little quiver for a second or two? Or while you were working on an important project, you suddenly *knew* you had to go to the bathroom right *now*!?

Well, let me tell you.

Just as sort of a *sideline*, your brain coordinates all of your body's physical activities—organ operations, temperature control, digestion and any bodily function we never think about. These are managed by a tiny control center deep within our brain.

When we scratch ourselves and bleed, that little control center rushes out white and red corpuscles, blood coagulants—whatever is needed for instant repair—just like ambulances roaring down the street to an accident. We can not consciously do what it does *automatically* and that is a twenty-four hour a day job. This tiny control center directs all of these vital procedures perfectly.

We don't do a thing. It does it *all*. Oh, excuse *me*! What a big error!

We're always responsible for its actions. What about the individual behind the wheel of an automobile racing along the road uncontrollably—guided by a *computer* unable to function properly—simply because its owner supplied it with a dangerous menu... either through the stomach or bloodstream?

Look in that mirror again.

I'm going to explain some things about 'computer language' which may be unfamiliar. It'll make you feel mighty good.

I use a Macintosh 650 Quadra computer. I get information from files, similar to a desk drawer with folders. One folder might contain insurance papers, another has house payments, another is for automobile papers, etc.

In the same way, a computer has a series of drawers (pigeon holes) where information is located. The name of the 'drawer' you want to open must be spelled correctly or the monitor (screen) simply writes "no matching items were found."

For example, *Disneeland* would be rejected. However, our minds realize Disneyland was supposed to have been written and we *see* hundreds of pictures all at once—Mickey Mouse, Pinocchio, the Seven Dwarfs—plus thousands of separate pictures of the characters in those stories. We can gather all kinds of information from our *computers* instantaneously... just from a single word!

The amount of material a computer can hold depends on its space for memory. Each chip holds just so much information and when it's filled, the monitor writes 'disk full.' However, *our computer* is the only one that never says disk full. Your *computer* can store all of the information found in all of the libraries in the entire world—and more. Maybe you should read that last line again, too!

At birth, our *computer* had only two items. Remember—every day we perform hundreds of thousands of activities, plus dream sequences. Oh yeah, wait till you learn about *them*. A fifty year old human has perhaps two-hundred-and-eighty quintillion bits of information stored in their brain.

Here comes another big eye-opener.

All computers locate information by *searching* through data banks (pigeon holes, drawers...).

Ask a computer—

(1) What is the population of Washington, DC?

(2) What is the telephone number of the White House?

(3) What is Santa Claus' address?

That plastic and silicon box will search for the answers and if they are not located, the screen reads: "it does not compute."

Well, good gracious. Isn't it strange that *we* didn't need to search? *Our computer* knew we did not have the answers to the first two questions and that it was *stupid* to ask for Santa's address! Our brain somehow knows what it does *not* know while the computer has to find out. Ask the computer the *same* thing five minutes later and it won't even remember you just requested the information a few moments ago. That magic box will dutifully begin its search all over again—even looking for the location of Santa's pad.

Oh, how about this:

(1) Who was Adam's wife in the garden of Eden?
(2) How many players are on a football team?
(3) What is the capital of Japan?

You didn't even *have to think*. The answers were automatic. The questions and answers are locked together. A computer would search several seconds, stumbling through many files, to reach the correct pigeon holes.

If a fifty year old person had to systematically probe two-hundred-and-eighty quintillion bits of information in this manner, it would require four *hundred* years to answer the question: "What is your name?"

Think about that, my dear friend, and realize you are a mighty important *something!*

I mentioned we began life with only two items in our computer. Actually they are two fears.

Fear of falling is one. Hold a little baby in your arms and quickly sink downward. The little guy will gasp for breath. We'll always be afraid of falling. It's a natural instinct. Although I am a pilot and love flying, I get weak and unsteady in a tall building next to an open window. You may chuckle at that confession, but just like that baby, you would gasp, too, if you felt yourself falling.

Next: fear of loud or unexpected noise. Let's go back to that little baby. Slap your hands in its face and see the body jerk, the fast squinting eyes, and hear the sudden loud cry. It's frightened!

We'll never outgrow those two fears. They're there for our own protection.

I n 1938, '39 and '40 Mickey Rooney starred in a series of Andy Hardy movies. He owned a Model A Ford roadster painted black and white with the initials AH! on the side of each door. I bought one and painted it just exactly like his.

After Jimmy Wakely moved to Hollywood, I wanted to visit him and two of my buddies and I decided to drive this little car out there after graduation. I remember Dad's prediction, "Babe, if you come back in that car, you'll be alone."

Cars passed us honking their horns and people waved seeing 'HOLLYWOOD or BUST' on our big homemade bumper sticker. It took us five days.

I wanted to stay awhile, so I found a place to live behind Grauman's Chinese Theatre and got a job washing dishes at the Ontra cafeteria near Hollywood and Vine. I worked every day from two until ten at night.

Jimmy and Inez gave me a party and the guests included the Sons of the Pioneers, and Gene Autry and his wife, Ina. *What an experience!*

O ne evening after my dish washing job, I walked down to the corner of Hollywood and Vine about 10:30. I stopped, looking toward Grauman's Chinese theatre and thought, "One day you'll stand here and people won't just walk by, they'll know you, Laverne. People will know who you are."

Thirteen years later, in 1954, at that exact spot, an

incident took place, and I'll tell you about it in another chapter.

Weekly amateur contests were held at the Million Dollar Theatre in Los Angeles and I entered with the Donald Duck act Mom and I had written so many years ago. I won, but it was a preliminary round and I had to return in two weeks.

At this same time, Mom and Dad called, telling me the state wide amateur contest was being held in Oklahoma City. I found four people going back there in a car and shared the expenses. I drove almost all the way and thankfully, I won first prize—a brand new *one hundred dollar bill*. I had never *seen* one, much less *owned* one. I was in shock, examining it when a very nice lady, one of the judges, spoke these unforgettable words:

"Laverne, you have a wonderful talent imitating Donald Duck, but had you not given that little three minute introduction in your own personality, you would never have received *my* vote. Let him take you as far as he can, but remember, it is *you* for whom I voted—not the duck. Don't forget that." I squeezed her hand and thanked her most sincerely.

I repeated the drive back to California with another group and returned to the Million Dollar Theatre, where again I won... $50.00.

Man, I was loving show business.

I also brought a letter of introduction to Walt Disney from the Oklahoma City Chamber of Commerce telling him I should become the "Stand By If Needed" Donald Duck.

I stood by, all right... I never was allowed inside

the gate at the Disney Studios. But wait—later on, Mr. Disney *did* learn who was out there.

Here's AH!—the little Ford I drove all the way to Hollywood and back... *ugh*... and after fifty years, there's no way on earth I could tell you who the little fella is I'm holding in my arms. That's Dad peeking around behind me.

8. "Greetings, Uncle Sam Needs You!"

Ominous clouds were gathering all around the world. England and Germany were fighting and rumors of our involvement were growing. I knew it was time to get home. Where were my two buddies? I haven't seen either one since we separated more than fifty-three years ago.

Dad was right. I drove home alone. It was the most frightening, desolate journey in my life, but he never made fun of me or said, "I told you so." It was a good lesson.

December 7th—Pearl Harbor. Bub and Moyne were attending Oklahoma University when the arrival of their familiar "Greetings, Uncle Sam needs you" telegrams shocked Mom so much. Bub was engaged to a beautiful student, Betty Finke, who he married, and to whom he is still married fifty-three years later. I was too young to be drafted, and started working as a truck driver for a plumbing contractor.

Bub came home telling how strict the Army was. Standing at attention, sergeants barking out orders, saluting officers. "Sir this." "Sir that."

I roared, "Man, that's the last straw. I wouldn't take that kind of crud, Bub!"

"I can't wait till they get *you* in the Army, you loud mouth little son-of-a-gun! You'll see!"

"No, I won't. They won't be able to do *me* that way!" Sounds like we hated one another, but no...

only brothers *talking* to each other.

When I was drafted a year-and-a-half later, Bub held the rank of Private First Class, yet I was promoted to Buck Sergeant three months and seventeen days after I was sworn in. *Whaaaat?*

Explanation:

After the formal induction—shots, examinations, issuance of supplies, etc.—I was shipped to Fort Sill, Oklahoma for basic training, exercise and learning how to march... known as close order drill. I ate this up. I learned the commands and even shouted them marching backwards at the side of units. A few weeks later we shipped out in all directions.

My destination was Camp Swift, Texas, where a new Combat Engineers Battalion was being developed. The First Sergeant looked like a bull dog. He lined us up the moment we arrived and shouted loudly, "Can anyone in this group type?" What a dumb question. I could run off a minimum of seventy-five words a minute.

I quickly learned you don't volunteer for anything in the Army. You await a *subpoena*. But I didn't know that when I screamed out, "I can, sir!"

Recall how I fussed at Bub for taking that "Army crud"? I wound up saying "sir," and saluting *anyone* who would talk to me.

He told me to come forward and I followed him to the office. Once inside, he pointed to a chair behind a typewriter sitting on a desk.

"Sit down. Your name, soldier?"

"Private Ivy L. Shinn, sir."

"Good. You are now the clerk typist, Private Shinn."

I was now the "what"? No audition. No test. I was

it. I hadn't even been asked if I *wanted* to be the clerk typist.

For the next two weeks, I typed everything imaginable: motorpool supplies, kitchen supplies, soldiers' names, their records, et cetera; and a whole lot *more* et cetera.

This big First Sergeant was 'hatched' in Illinois. After he saw me looking dolefully out the window one morning he asked, "What's the matter, Orange Blossom?" He thought my accent was more southern than anyone else.

I pointed to the passing soldiers and quietly answered, "I sure would like to go out there and lead that platoon in close order drill." His reaction to my simple confession was really something. He roared with laughter, which made me feel about as good as pouring salt in an open wound.

My desk was just outside the office of the Company Commander, who heard our conversation. He came to the door. "Do you really want to *try* giving some close order drill, Private Shinn?"

"Oh, yes sir, Lt. Wall. Please, sir!" I would have kissed his hand (almost) if it would have done any good.

"All right." I followed him... and *bull dog* was right at our heels. Lt. Wall stopped the next platoon. I gave him a snappy salute and took over. Remember, no one had ever heard me say a word. Clerk typists don't march. *They just type!*

I brought the platoon to attention and you could have heard me a block away. "R-i-g-h-t Face! For-w-a-r-d *M-a-r-c-h!* First squad to the rear march! Second squad to the rear march!" and I scattered them all over the area. I turned around—walking backwards now—yelling out the commands. My heart was pounding a mile a minute. Sneaking a peek at Lt. Wall, he was grinning *like Dad's cat* and I saw bull dog's teeth too, because his mouth was wide open and his eyes were bugging out a foot.

I issued several more snappy commands and, in about five minutes total time, had them halt.

I never saw that typewriter again!

As I said, this was a new Battalion of Combat Engineers. That's how I was promoted to Squad Sergeant so quickly. I happened to be at the right place—at the right time.

A USO troupe starring Red Skelton came to Camp Swift, and I emceed the show. Yes, even in the Army, I performed whenever and wherever possible.

I was performing before those soldiers doing close order drill... merely continuing my yell leading days in school.

B ub was a bomber ground crew chief. Moyne and I both dreamed of being pilots, but he didn't take the exam. You see, Moyne knew I would be in military service shortly, and since I had not been to college, he was afraid I couldn't pass the pilot's exam. And if I couldn't fly... he wouldn't either. *What a brother!*

However, after becoming Sergeant, I learned I *could* take the Air Force examination. Oh, I was excited and made the appointment. It was a test of 150 multiple choice questions.

If you didn't know the answer to a question, you could circle the number *of* that question with a zero.

For every five zeroes you received one point. In other words, for ten zeroes, you were given 2 points on the total score. Fifteen zeroes, 3 points, etc. The passing score was 69.

I was so nervous and the questions were difficult. I knew a few of them and smiled as I marked the correct answers. Those I didn't know for sure I *used that zero* and was the last one to finish. Everyone taking the test knew how much this meant to me because I had explained Moyne was waiting to see if I passed before he took it.

The examiner placed a sheet over my paper showing correct answers through little slots, and then shook his head. "I'm sorry. There's *no way* you have passed, sergeant."

"Sir, there are a lot of zeroes on my paper," I said hopefully.

He smiled, "There would *have* to be—but more than you could possibly have." So he laid my test aside and continued grading the others.

I couldn't leave. When he had finished grading all of them, he looked at me. "All right, sergeant, I will *count your zeroes.*" He had already counted my correct answers, and I only had a total of 59. Slowly he counted, his eyes getting bigger and bigger. I looked around the room and even those who had failed were still there, keeping their fingers crossed for me.

Then after what seemed like forever, I heard him almost whisper, "I can hardly believe this. You have fifty-five zeroes on this paper, which means you have eleven more points, for a total of 70. Passing is 69. One day you can tell your grand children you passed the Air Force examination by making *zero* instead of a hundred."

I couldn't wait to get to a phone and call Moyne. He was equally happy and of course, breezed through his test, too. We were both going to be pilots now. Wheeeeeeee!

I went to Norwich University in Northfield, Vermont for Air Force college training, where I had my first airplane ride, on skis no less.

Forty-eight hours before we were scheduled to leave for primary training, the Battle of the Bulge began. Immediately 36,000 cadets with previous ground or service forces training were returned to their respective branches for shipment overseas.

Bennie Barr, my old school buddy, was motorpool sergeant of Company Headquarters, 1270th Combat Engineers in Fort Smith, Arkansas. With his influence, I was transferred to Company C.

At Camp Chaffee, I soloed in a little J-3 Piper Cub by getting out to the airport as often as I could, since *flying* was in my veins.

TO WAR!

We were essential, so we were out of there as quickly as possible. Ohhh, that boat trip across the Atlantic! Sick... sick... sick! I'll *never* understand how anyone could be a sailor.

9. "Heah Ah Is, Honey Chile!"

Father Time raced on. Bub and Betty were married. Moyne was flying and had met his bride-to-be. Where was I? La Havre, France and our battalion was pushing its way across the land.

Each sound of P47's or 51's majestically sweeping overhead carried my eyes skyward, and I pretended I was there and not in soggy mud.

This was the Third Army Division with General George Patton conspicuously up front. Those pearl handled pistols dangling at his side rekindled my childhood movie memories.

I learned soldiers could wear 'side arms' if they came from home. Dad shipped me a pistol and holster he bought from the police chief. Boy, you should have seen that .45 calibre police special, nestled in the beautiful left-handed holster, hanging at my side. I imitated those cowboys I had seen as that little boy. Mickey Rooney starred in a visiting USO show, and I reminded him later in Hollywood that my gun had been part of his wardrobe. Our birthdays are the same... September 23rd.

I entertained whenever possible. Colonel Conners, the battalion commander, sent for me whenever entertainment was needed.

A letter from Mom and Dad changed my life. "Babe, Bub and Betty had a little boy. They wanted to name him Jimmy Weldon, but Bub said,

'No, we can't use one of Verne's names'." I thought, hmmm... Jimmy Weldon. I like that name... I *really* like that name. I told Mom and Dad to tell Bub and Betty how much I liked the name Jimmy Weldon and had adopted it *myself*... and should they ever have another son, please give it to him and I would do my best to make him proud of it. Well, there *is* a Jimmy Weldon Shinn who arrived a couple of years later. I tell everyone I was named after him *before* he was born! We're real pals.

Augustine Mandino is the greatest religious writer today. I've memorized his cassette tape of "The Greatest Salesman In The World." When he was in high school, he once abbreviated his name on an English paper: Aug. Mandino.

His teacher casually remarked, "That was a nice paper you turned in, Og."

He smiled, "Ma'am?"

She repeated, "Nice paper you turned in, Og." You see, she created a word from the sound of the *abbreviation* for Augustine. That comment captured his imagination, changing his name to Og Mandino. I learned this in 1986—forty-one years after Mom and Dad's letter had changed mine.

My battalion was ten miles from Czechoslovakia when the war in Europe ended. Colonel Conners went with me in *his* jeep to General Eisenhower's Command in Frankfurt.

"This soldier should have been in Special Services all along," he stated. I transferred to SHAEF Headquarters.

Jackie Richards Massaro was a member of this close-knit crew. I explained my new name as he grinned,

"You *are* Jimmy Weldon." These were my happiest months as a soldier.

We were given the opportunity of remaining to attend schools in Europe. As an actor, I didn't *need* college. Now, I'm shaking my head sadly reading that stupid remark.

"Look over the list. Maybe there's one you want to attend."

"No way," I shook my head.

"Just look, Jimmy."

"All right! Give me the list!"

I scanned these educational facilities, totally unimpressed, *until* I saw The Royal Academy Of Dramatic Arts in London, England.

I yelled out, "That's the one I want to go to!" Everyone fell out of their chairs laughing. I had selected the one school *nobody* could enter... they thought.

I flew to London and convinced the director, Sir Kenneth Barnes, of my sincerity—and he accepted me. I remained in the Army, assigned in London to attend RADA. I was given quarters in the neighborhood and ate my meals with a nearby Army group.

Just learn your acting skills now, "J.W."

At The Royal Academy of Dramatic Arts you are taught *theatre* only.

Fencing: not to be a swordsman, but to learn how to walk—and glide across the stage.

Speech: how to pronounce words. Man, did I need that class. I *still* do.

Wardrobe: knowing costumes; how to make them, why they were worn and when. You really *learn* about clothing.

Soliloquy: this gives an actor confidence to continue the scene when another actor forgets his or her lines. They help each other with what are known as 'ad libs.' This class proved to be so important while performing with the late Don Ameche in a play written *for* me.

Pantomime: acting with no dialogue.

Critiquing: giving a fellow actor your perceptions of what he did or did not do in a given performance. This is the class I spoke of in Chapter 4, watching the Our Gang movie.

Stage: the most extensive training is here; playing all sorts of roles in full costume. RADA's costume department is huge.

I was doing the balcony scene in Romeo and Juliet. Standing on stage, dressed in skintight pants, cape— the works—when I glanced up at this girl playing Juliet. She was gazing out over the stage, calling "Romeo, Romeo. Wherefore art thou, Romeo?"

I couldn't keep from thinking how funny I must look at that moment and blurted out

"Heah ah is, honey chile!"

I thought she was going to fall off of that makeshift balcony. Miss Fabia Drake, our instructor, was sitting down in the theatre and registered no humor.

"Jimmy Weldon, your accent is atrocious enough. Do it properly!"

"Yes, ma'am, Miss Drake," I meekly apologized.

I worked in a picture at Pinewood Studios, *Stairway to Heaven*, starring David Niven and Kim Hunter. And I believe this was the first picture for Richard Attenborough, now 'Sir' Richard, the renowned English director.

My scene was a bomber crew entering heaven through a doorway. The fellow in front of me was portraying an unhappy life, therefore heaven really was something special.

"Boy, home was never like this!" he smiled happily.

Following him, my portrayal was the opposite. Looking around sadly I confirmed quietly, "Mine was," then walked on through.

Big scene. Two words. "Mine was." However, I was as happy as if it had been the leading role.

....Mine was....

10. The Seventeen "Nones"

E ntertainment for the Allied Armies was held at Rainbow Corner, England's version of a USO canteen, and this was *the* spot every person in military service visited when they were in London.

In order to have enough hostesses to serve soft drinks and dance with these transients, it was mandatory that English show girls spend a scheduled number of hours there. I performed my Donald Duck act on stage every weekend.

Following my performance one Saturday night, I met a young lady serving soft drinks, Muriel Doreen Jones, and asked her to dance. She agreed, and I then had the *nerve* to tell her I didn't think she could dance very well.

In the following weeks we had several dates, and she invited me to her home to meet her family. Her parents were Horace and Dorothy, and her brother, Kenneth. Oh, by the way, a few weeks after our informal introduction, I enjoyed seeing "The Night and The Music" at the Coliseum, one of the longest running live shows in London. Muriel just *happened* to be one of The Four Pairs, the leading dance team. And I had said she couldn't dance.... Gollee.

As time passed, romance blossomed. However, stories of disenchanted English war brides returning home were common. I convinced her parents this would never happen to us. We would be married only *if* she liked both my family *and* America, so we rushed down to make the necessary arrangements.

At the American Embassy, I explained to the gentleman why I wanted Muriel to return with me, but not as my wife. He was very understanding and held up a form to fill out.

"Fine. Let's just get the information. First, what employment do you have in America?"

"I don't have a job now, sir. I just got out of the Army and have been going to school here."

"Oh?" Hesitating a moment, he then wrote the word *none* on the line.

"Do you have a house in America?"

"No, sir, I live at home with my parents." Another *none* was noted.

"How much money do you have in the bank in America?"

"Sir, I don't have any money in a bank anywhere."

Again, *none* was the only word necessary.

"What are your prospects for a job when you get home?" The silence and blank expression on my face were qualifications enough for him to pen still another *none*.

As these simple, important questions continued, both Muriel and I realized there was far more to 'it' than just 'boy, do I love you!'

To make a long story nauseating, seventeen *nones* were on this form... answers to questions appropriate for her authorization to enter America.

He shook his head with a pained expression, "I can't let this girl go to America."

I thought I had the answer. "Daddy will take care of her, sir."

But I wasn't thinking clearly. "Son, your *father* isn't

marrying her. *You* are."

We left, feeling like another favorite expression of Dad's—"as low as a toad's behind in a wagon rut." If you ponder that assessment, that is truly *low*.

However, by the time we arrived at her house we were excited again, and we outlined our plans for her parents.

"I'll go home and get my show business career started, then send for Muriel. If she likes it there, we'll get married. If not, I'll just send her home and no one is hurt. But if Muriel does marry me, we are going to stay married, and I promise she will come home to visit you!"

They were happy with our decision because they believed that after I left England the results would be: Absence makes the heart grow fonder... for somebody else!

They gladly waved, "Good bye, Jimmy."

Muriel's parents
The Duchess   and   Popski

73

11. *There's gotta be a reason!*

When I decided to remain overseas and attend RADA, I received my Army discharge, which meant I had to furnish my own transportation home.

Now, to verify the truth of those seventeen "nones" in the preceding chapter, I didn't have the money to buy a ticket on *anything*. Next, I want you to know I get seasick in a bathtub; nevertheless, I worked my passage back to America on a boat, as a 'wiper.' Uh, wiping up oil and grease in the engine room... ohhhhhh... ugh.

As soon as I got home, a radio station was going on the air in Chickasha. I hoped to become one of its announcers, but I wanted to go to Hollywood first, so out I went—with extreme enthusiasm.

My excitement faded rapidly, however, as I heard the same statement everywhere, "Don't call us, we'll call you."

I did receive the most valuable advice possible from Don Forbes, a CBS network radio announcer. "Jimmy, go back to Chickasha and develop something Hollywood doesn't have and they'll open their arms to you." Those were his exact words.

Pretty discouraged, I came home. Soon radio station KWCO was ready. I auditioned and got my first *show business* job—as an announcer. Remembering Don Forbes' suggestion, I dreamed up a disc jockey show using the duck voice. The manager gave me an

My first job in 1946 as an announcer at KWCO
where little Webster was found.

hour each afternoon to see how my idea would be accepted. I played records and talked to listeners on the telephone, playing their requests. The difference from other such shows was that this little duck wandered into the studio and talked to everyone on the air. Mom and her sister named him Webster Webfoot. The illusion was successful, because my listeners believed we were *two* people. Webster especially liked Spike Jones and other novelty records, and the amount of mail he received pleased the manager.

D ad posted a bond for Muriel to come to America because of those "nones" on our initial request. I'd been home almost a year when she finally arrived. Imagine leaving London, England—a city with hundreds of years of history—only to arrive in Chickasha, Oklahoma... a community which proudly boasted a two-hundred-and-fifty watt radio station. Dry, sticky, hot and miserable. Muriel had done just that. But happily, she decided to stay. In fact, she stayed at our house for five months. Mom asked me one night, "Babe, are you going to marry Muriel or not?" Frankly, I was scared to death.

I was Bennie's best man at his wedding in 1946, shortly after I came home. One Saturday night, Bennie, Dorotha, Muriel and I had dinner together, and on the spur of the moment decided to drive to Rush Springs, twenty miles south of Chickasha, where Muriel and I would get married. We did—September 26, 1947 at 11:00 pm—after calling the minister from a telephone booth and getting him out of bed. I tried to talk Muriel out of it, but she said she was staying. That's the truth. This took place three days after my twenty-third birthday.

Another radio station had just gone on the air in Duncan, forty miles south of Chickasha. I figured it was time for Webster to spread his wings, so Muriel and I moved there. The manager was Eddie Evans, a former announcer at WFAA in Dallas. After several months, he suggested that I audition for WFAA which would really be a big advancement. We drove to Dallas, and I was hired both as a staff announcer and children's entertainer. It was a fifty-thousand watt clear channel station. *Wow!* Our show was an hour each afternoon—the year, 1948.

The general manager, Martin Campbell, asked me to have a little Webster Webfoot puppet made because WFAA was moving into television and we were to be the children's program.

I had no idea what Webster might look like. I had only done the voice. However, using a combination of several suggestions, Webster was created.

It is far more difficult to *talk like a duck* than in a normal manner, and knowing that ventriloquists try to keep their mouths as still as possible, I was anxious to see how I was going to survive the test.

The first child who saw Webster was Moyne and Lorraine's little girl, Patti. She had heard 'him' on the radio, so when I walked in and knelt down by this little three year old, I was amazed at how quickly she accepted him as her friend—a live little duck.

Each time Webster talked, she looked straight at him. *I wasn't even there* as far as she was concerned. I also realized that when I talked *to* Webster, my looking at him automatically caused others to look at his reactions too, just as in any conversation. Most ventriloquists face the audience to display their ability to talk for the character without movement of their lips. I was not interested in showing such an ability. I only wanted children to think of little Webster as a real person.

Patti was thrilled when I told her Webster was three years old, just like she was. His birthday? February 31st. You see, he'll always remain three. After all, he knows his own birthday—or so he tells everyone.

WFAA purchased the TV station. When we had our audition, everyone whispered, "If this goes on the air, it won't last a week. Jimmy is the fair-haired boy of Martin Campbell."

We began April 4, 1950. Less than a week later, a call came to the studio from Dr. Abrams.

"Hello, this is Jimmy Weldon, what may I do for you?"

"I have a question which may seem silly, but it's not meant to be."

"Fine, sir. What is it?"

"Would you come down and give your life story to a hundred-fifty doctors and their wives?"

"Would I what?"

"Give us your life story. The reason I'm requesting this, I was sitting across the breakfast table from my wife this morning and asked, 'Darling, why am I a doctor? Think. There has to be a *reason* why I'm a doctor.'

"She answered, 'I don't know. Maybe you should see one.'

"I continued. Why is Phil, my best friend, an attorney?

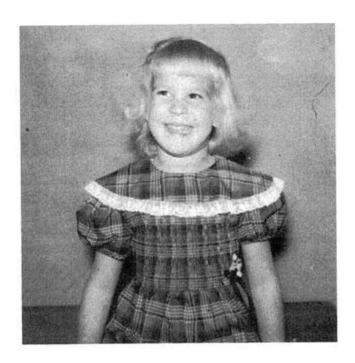

Webster's first little friend, Patti, still has that beautiful, capti-
vating smile and those bright, twinkling eyes she had at three.
Today, she has two beautiful daughters—Bobbie Jo and
Monica Lynn.

"She questioned, 'Why are you asking *me* why you are a doctor or Phil is an attorney?'

"I'm reading a story in the Dallas Morning News about a young man named Jimmy Weldon who's talking like a duck for a living. There's gotta be a *reason!* Would you please tell us?"

I did.

In closing my presentation, I took little Webster out of his suitcase, looked straight at my audience and declared, "This is the little guy I hope one day will take me to Hollywood." I did a routine and they laughed.

Dr. Abrams walked up to me and declared, "Jimmy, I'm not interested in *you*, but I'll buy any part of that duck!"

Ash Dawes, my first director, had a little girl named Pam, the same age as Webster. Three years old.

I was offered $150 to let Webster bite a stripper on the breast at the Dallas Athletic Club—a few seconds—for $150. I was laughing as I explained my cash windfall to Ash.

"Jimmy, don't you dare do it."

"What?"

"No, Jimmy."

"Why not?"

Ash reminded me that Webster was a real little person to the children.

"I know that, Ash. They'll be in bed at this hour. No child is going to see me."

"No, but the Moms will. Jimmy, don't ever let little Webster do anything that would destroy his personality with the children. Keep him a little three year old duck who understands how they think at that age. He's their friend."

Bless his heart, what a tremendous bit of advice. Today, more than forty-four years later, we have remained the best of pals. Ash has happily stated that he was one of those early believers, "That duck will last about a week... no more!"

To substantiate how real little Webster was to our viewers, the Bob Stanford show was broadcast each day one hour later. On Fridays, he aired *The Frito Kid*, sponsored by the Frito-Lay Corporation. Bob was the Frito Kid and his arch enemy was Snake Bit Sam, played by Easy Marvin. Easy later moved to Hollywood and was the announcer on an NBC network program with Webster and me.

Anyway, they dreamed up the bright idea that Snake Bit Sam would kidnap Webster and put him in an oven—to have roast duck. The switchboard lit up like a Christmas tree. Mothers were calling. Their children were screaming and crying, terrified that little Webster was being roasted alive.

Don't tell me children are *not* easily frightened. Re-read the opening lines of this book. *They are real!*

Bob was home watching the show when the studio called telling him pandemonium had erupted. He jumped in his car, hurrying to the studio. As soon as he arrived, he went on camera and apologized to the viewers.

"Little Webster is all right. He and Uncle Jimmy will be back tomorrow afternoon at their regular time, when Webster will tell you himself that Snake Bit Sam didn't hurt him."

We did exactly as Bob promised, and yet people

wonder today why there is so much violence and crime.

Remember Clark Gable's line, "Frankly, my dear, I don't give a damn!" in the picture *Gone With The Wind*? That was the most shocking language ever used in a film up to 1939. Today there are no words left out of movies. All of the violence, crime, sex and filth you can muster up is flashed on the screen. Our television shows make Sodom and Gomorrah look like a Sunday school picnic. No one cares anymore, and it's destroying our nation.

I used the term 'unrestricted television' as being basically wrong with today's adults in chapter one. May I go further? Thank you.

I have a dish in my back yard which brings into my living room all of the programs televised on satellites. Some of you reading this have no idea what is being shown through our skies. There is no such thing as a pornographic film. I want to laugh at that term. It's such a joke. Call it "spreading pure filth and degradation" and you have a good name.

It's a disgrace knowing government leaders can't tell the difference between *art* and pure *filth*, yet any mother can look at a picture and decide if it's one she does or doesn't want her children to see. Our ratings mean nothing. A "PG," "X," or *whatever*-rated film is no way to determine what's good or bad.

Producers of films keep stretching the envelope to show more junk, and then attempt to persuade everyone their material is strictly a promotion of art and free expression. The minds of our children are open for every single impression they receive. TV sets are our baby sitters, *or* they are being viewed by children whose *sitters* select the channels.

L ike my father, Ash Dawes has a deep insight. Forty-five minutes following Webster's show was a program called "Chalk Talk." An artist drew pictures on big sheets of paper with amazing speed and skill. Musical backgrounds depicting the mood of his drawings were selected so carefully. If the artist was drawing a picture of a happy scene, then light, airy, instrumental notes softly danced in the viewers' ears, subconsciously bringing an inward sense of genuine peace. On the other hand, if his drawing was a hostile, sinister concept of something, the most weird, foreboding musical combinations imaginable streamed through the speaker. This program contained no talk; only music and this fella's excellent talent. It was a very popular show, enjoyed by viewers of all ages.

One evening when he had finished work, Ash was leaving the studio and stopped for a second, listening to the music coming from the control room. It was absolutely the strangest he had ever heard. He glanced into the studio and saw the artist's completed picture—a witch standing at the edge of a hazardous precipice overlooking the seashore. The wind, whipping her hair and dress wildly, was bending the tall tree nearby and sending huge waves crashing on the rocks below. Everything in the photograph was ominous... yet good! Ash was impressed and smiled, giving a complimentary nod to the artist as he strolled to his car to go home.

Upon his arrival, he was greeted with hugs and

kisses from Betty and Pam. They enjoyed a delicious dinner and comfortably settled themselves in the living room to watch television.

Shortly thereafter, the mantel clock chimed the three year old's bedtime and custom continued—that being a good night tuck under the covers along with more hugs and reassurances she was loved very much.

Ash and Betty again returned to the living room to relax, check the news, etc. Naturally, anything originating from channel 8 studios was of extreme interest to Ash, for he was the production manager.

Perhaps ten minutes passed, when they were startled by a scream coming from Pam's bedroom.

Rushing in, Ash carefully gathered her in his arms as she cried, "Daddy, Daddy, that old lady was after me. Daddy, she was after me." Calming her and carrying her into the living room, he sat down holding her snugly. The moment she was truly awake, Ash quietly sought a description of her intended abductor. While she was trying to tell him, Ash suddenly remembered the "Chalk Talk" photograph.

He asked Betty if Pam had seen the show, but she didn't know. At that time, she was in the kitchen preparing dinner. Following a few more questions and Pam's description, Ash said, "Don't let her go to sleep, Betty!" and rushed to the door.

"Ash, where are you going?" Betty called out frantically.

"Just keep her awake, sweetheart!" was all she heard, as he rounded the corner to the garage.

It was a twenty minute journey each way. Ash hoped to locate the one item he was positive would restore Pam's *computer*. He leaped from the car at the back entrance to channel 8 as nimbly as a teenager.

In a wild frenzy, he emptied the huge drum containing all of the used paper, praying the single parchment he was searching for would be among the pieces. It was. He rolled it up and raced back to the car and home, with Betty still at a loss at his hurried departure.

"Is Pam still awake?"

"Of course, Ash. She's in the living room watching television. Where have you been?" She tried to keep up with his steps to Pam.

Ash had already reached her by the conclusion of Betty's question. Kneeling on the floor, Ash unrolled the picture which had held his attention a few hours earlier. "Pam, is this that old lady who was chasing you?"

Her little eyes opened wide. "Yes, Daddy, that's her. That's her."

Ash spent plenty of time... *plenty of time...* explaining that it was only a picture drawn with some chalk. The same kind she played with there at home.

Moreover, his plan included further actions. They both sat there and playfully ripped the picture to pieces. Again Ash explained to Pam that it was just a picture made with chalk. Returning to bed, this time only pleasant dreams swirled through her little *computer.*

Oh, but wait! About a month later during another family television time, a similar photograph appeared on the screen and Pam jumped up quickly.

"Daddy, that looks like the old lady who was after me. But it was all play-like, wasn't it?"

"Yes, Darling. It surely was," Ash smiled, gently

stroking her hair.

Today, few fathers would even consider qualifying their child's nightmare, much less carry out the actions of Ash Dawes forty-four years ago.

"It was all a damn dream. Now go to sleep and be quiet!" is the compassion for most children, I sadly maintain.

I n chapter seven, we explored some facets of this unbridled *computer* we were given at birth. Let's go a bit further.

This three pound jelly-like machine stores everything we see, think and feel, and will return anything that's placed in it. It started with nothing in the beginning, yet through years of development, it has created architecture, music, books and poetry, the search for understanding of the basic truths and principles of the universe, life and morals—and likewise, it's responsible for bigotry, greed, hatred *and* whatever else is stored in it.

Think of how versatile this machine is. The one which directs the actions of a powerful football running back during Sunday afternoon's game may also be the unit guiding his hands across the piano keys playing soft music that evening. Or one who is in charge of delivering lectures to an assemblage of college students may find itself governing the repair of a child's tricycle tire the next day.

Computers made of silicone and metal can't set goals. They don't express ideas. They can't share their treasures, become curious or enjoy a sense of humor. No, these plastic boxes are emotionally barren, and when they're left alone, they can do nothing but sit

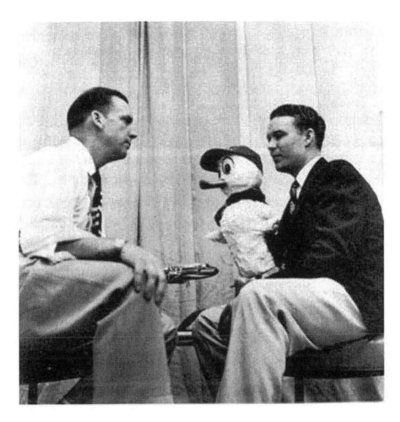

Ash Dawes, our first director, discussing something for our show. Yep, imagine seeing him race to the studios to locate a single photograph made of chalk. *Whatta guy!*

quietly, waiting for someone to feed them electricity and request the data they contain.

Will a computer ever understand the meaning of a disgusted look, a sarcastic remark, the soft touch of two lovers holding hands? How could a computer possibly grasp the meaning of death?

Yet, the most important difference between a metal computer and *ours* is its ability to communicate with itself. What part of the brain, for instance, can bring forth a particular memory, perform a specific action, or execute a computation?

Can we pinpoint this place of automatic response, or locate that tiny little control center that issues the commands? No. This is that unique part of man which places him at the side of no other living creature. Man is a thinker. No computer will ever announce, "I calculate... therefore, I exist."

Now suppose we take a peek at determining why so few of us are motivated by dividing the word *motivation* itself: motiv/ation.

Think about it. You won't even crawl out of bed without a motive, so let's make it *motive*/ation.

Continuing with logic, it's reasonable to assume the idea of getting up remains only a thought until you actually place your feet on the floor. So, let's add 'c', making it motive/*action*. That combination means doing what you *think* you can do and *want* to do.

When I speak in locations where the meal is self-service smorgasbord, I ask my audience to think like children. I point to the food. "When we were told the food was ready, what is the only reason we walked over there?"

They look dumbfounded as I continue, "Tell me. Think... honestly like a child. What is the *only reason* we went over *there*?"

Again, I point to the table holding the food and carefully stress those same three words.

Invariably someone will call out, "Because we were hungry."

When I shake my head and say, "No, that's not the reason," perhaps I'll hear, "Because they told us to!" Again I shake my head. No.

I then give them the startling truth. "The only reason we went over there is because that's where the food is. Not one person left the room when we were told, 'Go get your food.'

"Motivation is a desire held in expectation with the belief that it will be realized. You went over there because you knew that if you *did*, you would get something to eat. Period." It's that simple.

Everything we've ever done or ever will do is based on this premise: I want that and I'm going to get it. Nothing more, nothing less. It's such a shame that only one human out of every twenty is motivated. We have already discussed several reasons why that's a fact in earlier chapters.

I have a lot more to tell you about this fascinating *computer* each of us owns, perhaps including some startling maybe-you-are-not-aware-of facts.

I met Hal Kirk Biard, affectionately known as Aitch, who became my producer, writer, everything.

The Ideal Toy Company made a Webster Webfoot doll, and it was dreadful. You would never have known it was supposed to be Webster without the name on the label, but my old partner, Mom, developed a good one.

Bub checked into rubber molds and duplicated an exact likeness of Webster's head, while Moyne began a silk screening business, designing Webster Webfoot towels, cardigans, T-shirts, and caps—and selling hundreds of dozens.

The Webster Webfoot Show was the longest running television show in the Dallas/Fort Worth area with the same sponsor, the Sanger Brothers Department Store. Little Webster called it "Mister Sanger Brothers."

Webster's visit with Kate Smith in New York City, January 1951.

Ed Sullivan visited Dallas and was our guest in early 1952.

Each week, we had officers giving safety hints about school crossings, using animals and all sorts of ideas.

12. At Last... Hollywood!

We usually had nine or ten guests on our show ranging from three to twelve years of age and seated on two tiered rows in a little bleacher-type area. I want to share two events that happened during early television—*when everything was live!*

On the third day, I was introducing the first guest to Webster when the little boy at the far end raised his hand.

"Do you want something?"

"Yes, Uncle Jimmy," he said with a rather painful expression, "I want to pee." Well, as you can imagine, I nearly fell over. The parents were sitting in another room, yet their laughter was so loud it came clear through the walls.

"Okay, uh, go on out there, (I pointed to the exit), and when you're through... come on back." Golleeee, I didn't know what else *to* say.

Ash had a cameraman following the little fella through the door holding his hands over the front of his trousers searching for that rest room. This was precious and the parents' comments were priceless. However, the wonderful revelation (if I may use that word) is that none of our young visitors giggled. They felt their little companion had been respectful by requesting permission to leave, rather than just thoughtlessly walking out. In other words, he has gone now, so let's continue with the show. And you know—they were right.

I visited with our guests at least fifteen minutes before each program, getting them primed to meet
Webster. We practiced singing our courtesy and safety
song, said our names loud and clear, and just sort of
got to *know* one another.

Seated at the far end on the bottom row were the
headliners of this next episode—two brothers. The
little one sat quietly. I couldn't get him to say anything... not even his name. He was four years old,
but the older brother, who was six-and-a-half, was a
walking encyclopedia, thank goodness.

The last segment of our show was devoted to safety
and courtesy hints. One day a little boy had announced, "Uncle Jimmy, my safety hint is don't stand
on the Johnny when you brush your teeth. You might
fall in."

But back to *this* program now. I noticed when the
brothers came in the studio that the older one was
limping slightly. During the show, I talked mainly to
the younger one, hoping to break through somehow.
I was confident he wasn't nervous, he just wasn't going to talk. Okay, time for safety and courtesy hints.

His big brother proudly stated, "Uncle Jimmy, my
safety hint is be careful when you're playing in the
backyard barefooted. You might step on a nail."

Oh-oh. I quickly thought that that might be the
reason for his limp.

"Did this ever happen to you?"

"Oh yes. Just the other day."

"Show us."

"What?"

"Show us right now. Let's see where the nail stuck
in your foot."

The blood drained from his little face like you had used a siphon hose. I can understand his thinking: "Oh, is my sock clean? Is there a hole in it? Is my foot clean?" I can remember wondering the same things when I was his age.

He started taking off his shoe real slowly... then his sock... all the while looking back and forth at me and his foot. Well, the bottom of his foot was as clean and perfect as the day he was born. He swallowed and gulped, "Wrong foot." Bless his heart, he was so nervous, he'd forgotten which foot was hurt.

Now the little brother became a tiger. "What's the matter with you? It was your other foot! I was Tonto and you were the Lone Ranger. We were running through the back yard and you stepped on that board with the nail and...." He lost all inhibitions and was reliving that adventure. Unfortunately, the stage manager signaled that we were out of time. We ended the show listening to *Tonto* raving and the *Lone Ranger* still trying to take off the right shoe to show us his nail-stuck foot. Yes, little brother truly captured our hearts. What an ending to a show. Wow!

Two years later, Jimmy Wakely was performing in the Sportatorium. I had to see him.

Webster was appearing each day at the Dallas Fair, so I rushed out after finishing our last show and arrived about ten minutes before Jimmy's performance.

Jimmy was talking to the announcer, who looked up, saw me, and asked, "Hey! What are *you* doing here tonight?" I quickly explained our long friendship, as Jimmy stood still, sort of stunned.

Then the announcer asked, "Is Webster in your

car?"

"Yes!"

He turned to Jimmy. "If he introduces you, it'll be the best one you can have! He's the hottest personality in the Dallas/Fort Worth area, and they love his little duck."

He turned back to me. "Go get Webster. Hurry!"

This all happened so quickly that Jimmy had said nothing during that conversation. In fact, he was having difficulty following what was going on as I ran out to the car, got Webster, and rushed out on the stage upstairs from the ramp. When everyone saw Webster they went wild. I was so excited I could hardly stand it.

"You have no idea what this moment means to me. The man I am going to introduce encouraged me to be in show business when I was twelve years old, or I probably wouldn't be standing here now."

Webster broke in, "Who is he? Who is he?" They laughed.

"Webster, you were just a little goose then." He bit my nose scolding, "Stop that! I am a duck!" Again they roared with laughter and applause.

"I was living in Chickasha, Oklahoma and rode the bus to Oklahoma City, where I spent the night in his home. The next morning, I was a guest on his radio program at WKY. Ladies and gentleman, it gives me the greatest honor I could possibly have to ask you to welcome one of the finest cowboy and recording stars in Hollywood today... Mr. Jimmy Wakely."

As he came up, I started to run off the stage with Webster.

He grabbed me and whispered, "Don't leave." For

the next forty-five minutes I stood there as he entertained the audience and played to Webster and me.

It had been seventeen years since I first met this man, yet, at that moment, it seemed only a day. He finished his performance, and we left the stage.

"You'll be in Hollywood with me in two weeks. What is your name again now, Laverne?"

We hugged each other and laughed.

Dear friend, in the last chapter I continued search ing deeper into this powerful *computer* each of us owns. Just now, while reliving that moment so vividly more than forty-two years ago with Jimmy Wakely, my mind flashed to a little lady I met in 1974. I want to relate the story and explain my reason for placing it here in my book.

John Ascuaga asked me to come to Sparks, Nevada and speak to his employees. He's the owner of the Golden Nugget, which is open twenty-four hours a day, so I spoke three different times.

This is the only company I have had the privilege of visiting whose owner paid his employees to hear my presentation.

On the main casino wall are full color pictures of them. Yes, he does value their loyalty, giving each of them special recognition. He is home every evening with his family for the dinner hour, also. What a gentleman.

At one of the sessions, I watched a little lady in a pink uniform standing at the very back, off to one side. She was definitely interested in my presentation because she gave her full attention the entire time. After everyone had gone, she slowly made her way to the area where I was arranging materials and erasing the blackboard.

As I turned she said quietly, "Mr. Weldon, may I please shake your hand?"

The stage was elevated perhaps two feet above the floor where she was standing, and I knelt down on one knee, "Oh yes, ma'am, you certainly may. And I thank you for asking me that."

A smile came over her face. "Thank you for talking to *me*. I am a maid in the west wing and all I do is clean the commodes, but they are the cleanest in all of the building."

I held her hand. "I'm sure they are."

She moved away, but looked back confidently. "I *am* important. Thank you so much."

The tears rolled down my cheeks. She needed that special touch from someone.

She moved through the door, paused again and looked back once more. "Yes, Mr. Weldon, *I am important*. Thank you again for coming."

I stood there alone in the room. Quietly I whispered, "Thank you, Heavenly Father, for giving me something to say which does have meaning to people. Please never let it appear so memorized that they doubt my sincerity."

When I got back home, I wrote these words on a piece of Teletype paper about three feet long and stapled it across the wall above my desk so I could read it every day:

Jimmy, you are a motivator... not a preacher. Have fun with your presentations, and never forget that people want to laugh. Leave them excited about themselves and their futures. Every presentation must be new to you, as they have not heard it before. Remember how you, Jimmy Weldon, felt in 1964 when you first learned your personal worth. All must feel this!

My mind spins now, wondering who may have been responsible for planting the seeds in that little lady's mind. What kind of home did she have as a child? Did she have any help building her personal self image during those young years? Oh, the importance of a loving hand to hold, a father to respect and admire, so many intangibles a child must sense in the family environment. I remember as though it were this morning how my mother was so encouraging and confident of my pursuing the field of entertainment. I think of Ash Dawes and the picture he had to find for Pam at the age of three, and all of the parents who truly are there for their children when it is so very, very important.

There's a public service spot on television which runs now and then, and its contents are something to the effect: What a shame it is to waste a mind.

Okay, back to the Sportatorium and Jimmy Wakely. He wasn't joking. In less than two weeks, I met with MCA in Hollywood, and then following a series of other meetings, The May Company in Los Angeles announced, "Hurry on back to Los Angeles. We will sponsor you."

Webster began in Hollywood the first week in September, 1952, on KLAC-TV, channel 13, where little Webster's most ardent admirer met us through his TV set—Mark Hurlbut. At fifty-one, he and Webster still enjoy conversations on the phone today.

13. Income Never Reported

O ur producer was George Tibbles, who later wrote
My Three Sons for fourteen years. He also wrote
several dinner theatre plays: one for Kathy Crosby,
Maury Amsterdam, Imogene Coca and Sid Caesar,
Caesar Romero and one for *me*, which Don Ameche
and I did together. More on that one later.

Another marvelous surprise was learning that Don
Forbes was employed at channel 13, and he was very
happy to meet Webster—a creation which was the
direct result of his advice in 1947. He even directed
some of Webster's shows at that station. Isn't life won-
derfully strange and exciting?

A itch arrived in California and we really harmo-
nized as a team. Every day he gave me a list of
things to do, which I carefully carried out. I drove to
all of the May Company stores and visited with each
employee in the children's department. I kept them
informed on Webster's activities so that our viewers,
visiting the stores, would consider each employee
Webster's personal friend.

And it worked!

Every store sold Webster's caps, cardigans, sweat-
ers, T-shirts and towels, all of which Moyne produced
in Anadarko, as well as the dolls Mom, Dad and Bub
manufactured in Chickasha.

Each children's department had a Webster Webfoot club headquarters. Even junior high students

joined Webster's club and wore his club pin on their clothes. At our first personal appearance, more than five thousand visited Webster.

Betty White had Clarence Nash as a guest one day—the voice of Donald Duck himself. Her producer asked if Clarence would stay and be on Webster's show, which followed Betty's. I was surprised when the producer told me Clarence was angry.

"Hell no, I won't be on his show! I started with this duck before he was born, and now I go into junior high schools with Donald and hear, 'That's not Webster Webfoot'!"

A salesman suggested that the Donald Duck line of beverages advertise on the Webster Webfoot show. Walt Disney's defiant comment was, "Don't mention his name in this office again!"

Remember my standing outside the gate to meet Walt... waaaaay back in 1941? Chapter 7.

Webster was nominated the outstanding children's show in 1952, '53 and '54. He served as the Grand Marshal in many parades; perhaps the most notable was the 1953 Huntington Park Christmas parade.

I not only *promised* Muriel's parents she would visit them, she was there on her sixth trip when the following meeting took place.

It was Christmas time in 1954, and at about 8:45 a friend and I were walking on Hollywood Boulevard nearing Vine street. My *computer* suddenly triggered a thought. "You know, George, it's funny."

"What, Jimmy?"

"When I was seventeen, one night I stood right there (I was pointing to the northwest corner of the intersection of Hollywood and Vine) and I thought to myself, 'Some day people won't just pass by you, they will know who you are.'"

"Yeah, just think... You've been nominated three years in a row as the outstanding children's program in the Los Angeles area."

By now, we had almost crossed Vine. A drug store was on the corner then and, so help me God, a man, his wife, little boy and girl came out the door, and the little girl pointed excitedly, "Daddy, there's Webster Webfoot's father!" Tears flowed down my cheeks as she ran to me. "May I have your autograph, Uncle Jimmy?"

I knelt, hugging her little body, "Yes, darling, you may have anything I have on this earth."

Her father whispered to George, "What's wrong with him?"

"If you'd heard what he was telling me just a few minutes ago, you would understand," was George's soft reply.

14. The Day I Became a Bull Frog

I will admit that this chapter's title does create a little curiosity. 'What in the world does Jimmy mean?' Trust me, you won't be disappointed with my *mysteriousness*.

We all have nicknames. I began calling Muriel *Ring* in London. Don't ask me why. It was just a silly thing. Everyone in the family adopted it. Dad, Mom, Bub, Betty, Moyne, Lorraine and their children all called her *Aunt Ring*.

Speaking of Muriel... She was dancing at the Moulin Rouge on Sunset Boulevard and was continually working in films as an actress. She considered herself as an extra only, but she did several bit parts, and her English accent was as noticeable as my southern sounds. She decided to test her nerves and skill behind the wheel of an automobile, and became an excellent driver.

By now, my whole family had realized California was a great place to live and they joined us there. Moyne's family lived one block south of Muriel and me. Dad was such a *rooted Texan*—having migrated to Oklahoma—but he and Mom had lived here only two weeks when he said, "I can't believe anyone from Texas or Oklahoma ever lost anything they would want to go back there and find." California weather absolutely was *heaven on earth*, in his mind.

I remember that when I was back in Oklahoma, we either froze all day and all night or burned up with the heat twenty-four hours a day, all depending on the month of the year. Or we were in the cellar waiting for a tornado to go by. Back there, they talk about earthquakes in California. Good lands alive! They encounter floods, tornados, uh....

Nuf sed.

B arbara and Milton Merlin were the writers of *The Millionaire*, starring Marvin Miller. They also wrote *Halls of Ivy* for Ronald Colman and his wife, Bonita Hume. *Halls of Ivy* began as a radio program and one character, Calhoun Gaddy, was deleted from television scripts because they hadn't found an actor to play the role.

Well, one afternoon the family was watching Webster Webfoot, and they all felt my personality just about matched that southern gentleman. The entire Merlin family came to the studio, and Barbara declared confidently, "He *is* Calhoun Gaddy." I read the script they had chosen for this episode, and I was so excited.

Here's a description of the very first scene we filmed. I had to walk to the opening of a doorway and greet Ronald Colman (Doctor Hall) who was seated on a bench.

My line was only two words: "Doctor Hall."

What an amazing coincidence. Eight years earlier I had walked through a doorway in London to say two words: "Mine was." At that time, all I did was look around and remember how happy my life had been before I died.

Now there I was, once more standing in a door-way with only two words to say, but these were the beginning of a co-starring role with Ronald Colman, who was sitting less than ten feet in front of me.

"Quiet in the studio!" came a loud voice.

"Roll it!" was barked out.

"Marker!" another voice yelled.

Then the director called, *"Action!"*

"Doctor Hall." I smiled.

The director yelled, *"Cut!"*

I was startled. "I'm sorry, sir." I thought surely I had done something wrong.

I will repeat what I've said hundreds of times. We don't think in sentences; we think in *blocks of time*. At that moment, my entire life flashed before me: I saw that little girl lying on that floor after being hit with the beer bottle; my running out of the theatre screaming; Mom explaining *acting;* learning the duck talk; the amateur contests; RADA; Webster's creation; and now... Ronald Colman. I'd seen his name at RADA. *In that single moment,* I fulfilled every dream in my life.

The director smiled, "No, no, Jimmy. Do exactly as you did," and then called to a lighting man, "Give me a scrim over his right eye."

I bounded out of bed the following days. Each scene was more exhilarating than the last. The word *action* was beautiful music to my anxious ear, and if Muriel were here this minute, she would agree. Those truly *were* my happiest *working days...* ever.

Webster's success proved to be his downfall. What? Yes, that's true.

Channel 13 had the first television shopping program, and the sales department sold one hour every afternoon to the May Company. The minute I heard this report from one of the salesmen I went to Mr. Fedderson and announced, "You just ruined everything." He was dumb-founded. He gave Webster credit because of the success the May Company had from our show, but no one could visualize the ultimate outcome, other than Aitch and me.

Remember how, from the very beginning of the sponsorship, Aitch and I kept such close contact with the children's department personnel?

Suddenly, telephones were ringing throughout the chain, and store operators transferred the calls to the proper department for the callers' needs. But many people calling the store now simply said, "I want that item I just saw on TV."

"What item you just saw on TV?" was the operator's confused response.

"They said to call right now and get this special price."

"I'm sorry. I have no idea what you're talking about. Will you please hold the line?"

It was mass confusion! Havoc reigned in 1954! The May Company frantically attempted to correct the mistake of *not thinking this out clearly before implementing such an idea,* but it only created more chaos.

The program was cancelled after less than a month, and I knew the trickle-down effect would eventually end Webster's sponsorship as well.

We appeared at a benefit in Brentwood, the exclusive residential area of movie stars. As I was driving up, Keenan Wynn announced on a bull horn, "Webster Webfoot and Uncle Jimmy are just arriving and will be putting on a show in the hall."

Jeff Chandler and Randolph Scott gathered the children's tickets as they came in. They grinned, "You are much bigger stars in the eyes of our own children than we could ever be."

Ralph Edwards was present at this event and thrilled me with, "Jimmy, I would like to talk to you about doing a children's show on the NBC network."

I later met with him, and *Funny Boners* was developed, which Webster and I emceed every Saturday morning. Remember Snake Bit Sam in chapter 11? This was the show we did together, in 1955.

Addendum: Ralph Edwards is Chairman of the Board of the Pacific Pioneer Broadcasters. Several of us were in a van April 11th riding through the beautiful area near Solvang where our board meeting was held. We were reminiscing, and I reminded him of our earlier conversation. Ralph shook his head, "Yes, Jimmy, that was some time ago, wasn't it?" [This was 1994, and it had been almost forty years.]

Time escapes so quickly! I repeat: *Spend* it wisely, for it's impossible to *save*.

Here is my dear friend Aitch, Hal Kirk Biard, who really was responsible for Webster's success on TV. After *Funny Boner's* ended, CBS recruited his talents and Aitch became an executive with the network for 26 years, serving as Director of Information Services, Promotion Manager, Publicist, Trade Planter and Copy Editor.

Aitch is pictured with Dr. Frank Stanton, former president of CBS, Inc.

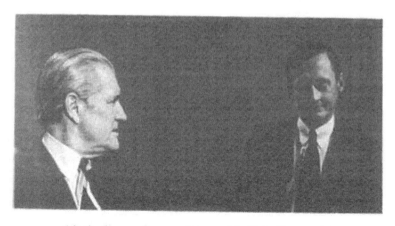

Aitch discussing an item with Eric Sevareid.

15. The Paradigm Effect

Bob Klein, a salesman at channel 13 when we came out here, had moved and was now sales manager for channel 8 in Fresno. He asked me to bring Webster up there, and we began our show September 5, 1956. I bought a Cessna 170 airplane and flew it all over the San Joaquin Valley. I often gave rides to our little viewers as a special prize for contests.

I met Cliff Ruby, the Mode O' Day supervisor for the San Joaquin Valley stores.

"Do you think Webster could sell women's dresses?" He believed the mothers watching the show with their children were potential buyers for themselves. I agreed—as long as a lady demonstrated the merchandise.

Now dear friend, I'm going to explain something which is an important part of our personality—our attitude. The very basic way each of us thinks. At first, it may sound silly, but please stay with me. The truth is almost unbelievable.

Here we go.

It's so easy to say *no* to a new idea. After all, anything *new* means we have to *change*. We ordinarily don't mind if someone *else* changes, but leave *us* alone. *Don't rock the boat.* This kind of thinking causes corporate executives to reject good ideas at board meetings, because eventually everyone ends up agreeing that the future is just an extension of the past. In other words, the ideas that got us this far are the

Webster and I are with a little guest who won an airplane ride in one of our contests. This was the Cessna 170.

ones we should keep to carry us into the future.

Galileo ran into the same thing in Venice in the 16th century. Every scholar believed the *Earth* was the center of the universe and not the *sun*. In order to prove they were wrong, Galileo took these leaders to the tower of San Marcos. With his new telescope, he proved his theory. He carefully presented documented evidence from his discoveries at night.

Now think about this. Galileo's facts were absolutely undeniable. He had incontrovertible proof that was the exact opposite of the thinking of these 'opinions of authority'—if we may call them that. These guys were mentally torn to pieces and agreed to torture Galileo if he didn't admit he'd made a mistake. Imagine... That actually happened.

Well, thank goodness Galileo's idea was finally accepted as fact, but a question remains. Why is there such overwhelming resistance to change? What blocks our understanding, acceptance and awareness of new ideas?

It all has to do with *paradigms*. The dictionary says a paradigm is a pattern or a model. They establish boundaries; they are the edges, the borders.

All right. That's enough background information on the word "paradigm" itself. Hang onto your seat because here are some eye-openers.

I took part in an experiment using a deck of cards. Eight cards were flashed individually on a screen, each for only a fraction of a second. The instructor said, "Concentrate and identify each card you see." It was really difficult because each looked almost like a blur. They were flashed four times, doubling the length of viewing time at each repetition.

A strange thing occurred. When seeing them the fourth time, we began to *sense* something was wrong, but we couldn't understand what was *bothering us*.

Here's what had taken place. The instructor had reversed the color of four of the eight cards. The red King of Hearts was now black, the Queen of Spades was red, the nine of Hearts was black and the six of Spades was red. As you know, the similarity in Spades and Hearts is very close. The big difference in the shape of Diamonds and Clubs would have been obvious if the colors of those suits had been transposed.

Again, seeing the red King automatically made us *think* it was the King of Hearts. Then too, the speed with which these cards were flashed focused our attention on the color and basic shape, nothing more. Continuing then, seeing a black nine, we assumed it was the nine of Spades, etc.

Had the instructor said, "I'm going to exhibit eight cards on the screen rapidly which have been altered somewhat. Watch carefully to detect these changes," we would have been looking for the deceptions. As it was, many of us never did *see* the differences and were embarrassed to discover our *locked in* paradigms.

Now, that's a good example of how a paradigm behaves in a recreational way. Wait until you read about *the following truth*.

For more than one hundred years, the Swiss were the most distinguished watchmakers on the face of the earth. In 1968 they were selling sixty-eight percent of the watches sold, and that meant more than eighty percent of the profits of worldwide sales. That is definitely 'market domination.' Yet, ten years later, this had plummeted to below ten percent, and they had to terminate fifty thousand of their sixty-five thousand watchmakers.

Do you know who is leading the watchmaking industry today? Japan. In 1968 they didn't have any market share. How on earth could the Swiss—known for excellence and innovations to their products—be so rapidly destroyed? Well, the answer is painfully simple. They were put back to zero by a paradigm shift. Many of you reading this right now own that *shift* and wear one on your wrist.

The quartz watch.

Think about it.

It's completely electric and a thousand times more accurate than the mechanical watch it replaced. It is battery powered and amazingly versatile. The one I'm wearing right now is a Casio musical watch which plays a different song every day of the week, plus Happy Birthday, two versions of the wedding march, Jingle Bells and—yeah, a lot more.

I promise I'm telling the truth. It actually *deserves* to be the new paradigm of time keeping. What a brilliant idea this is. Now, would you like to know who invented this marvelous machine? If you don't know, you're going to be impressed.

The quartz watch was invented by the Swiss themselves in their research laboratories. Yes, that is a fact. When the researchers presented this idea to the Swiss watch manufacturers in 1967, it was rejected. After all, it didn't have any bearings, there were no gears... why, this stupid thing didn't even have a main spring. There's no way it could possibly be the future of watches. The Swiss manufacturers were so confident that this would *never-get-off-of-the-ground*, they didn't even patent the idea.

Later that year, their researchers displayed this quartz watch to the world at the annual watch congress. Texas Instruments of America and Seiko of Japan walked by, took one look, and the rest is history.

Now, why couldn't the Swiss take this wonderful invention that *their own people* had created and run with it? The answer: the strength of paradigms again. They were blinded by the success of their old paradigms. When they were presented a profoundly new and different way to continue their success into the future, it was rejected because it didn't fit the rules at which they had always been so successful.

This factual report is not limited to the Swiss alone. It is the story about anyone, any organization, any nation who believes what has been successful in the past must continue to be successful in the future.

When a paradigm shift occurs, everyone goes back to zero. Your successful past doesn't guarantee you a thing in the future if the rules change. Not even the best watchmakers in the world could stop time. In fact, if you are not careful, your successful past will block your vision to the future. That's why you must develop an openness to new ideas, an eagerness to explore different ways of doing things, because only through that kind of open-mindedness can you keep your doors to the future wide open.

Surely, you remember that in the '60s we were convinced that low cost fuel would last forever. We said four children make up the ideal family. Cable television was a hoax; it would never become reality. And Japanese products would always be junk.

Were we ever wrong! Wow!

And we were mistaken because our paradigms prevented us from perceiving reality.

Knowing the power of our brains (to which I always refer as *computers*), we now discover they filter incoming experiences and pick out whatever best fits our rules and regulations and throw out the rest. Can you see how we develop bigotry, hatred and greed just as easily as we develop our good traits? Each is molded in our *computer* in the same manner.

Let's return now to my meeting with Cliff. He and I were excited about the prospects of sponsorship, but the paradigms of Mode O' Day's corporate headquarters' executives were exactly those of the Swiss watch manufacturers. They rejected it immediately. They didn't even want a discussion. Forget it! Cliff decided to sell his idea to the individual store owners. They accepted his enthusiasm for this different kind of merchandising, *and away we went.*

Well, dear friend, it didn't take long for sales to literally zoom in the Mode O' Day stores within our viewing area. You know without my saying, Cliff and I were grinning—yeah, *like Dad's cat.*

When the results were noted by the executive board, it almost became *their* idea. Mode O' Day was our longest continual interrupted sponsor. Interrupted, due to my behavior.

Cliff's wife was *Aunt Berniece,* who demonstrated Mode O' Day merchandise and helped Webster and me with other segments of the show.

Our relationship, which began about the middle of 1958, was suspended in January of 1959, when we became hosts of *The Hi Mom Show*, replacing Shari Lewis, on NBC's flagship station KNBC, in New York City.

Moving to New York was my life's biggest single blunder. That place is something else! Sorry, but I found absolutely no pleasure as one of its residents. I *had* to get out of there—and fortunately, channel 13 in Los Angeles let us return. By the way, did you ever hear of *The Muppets*? Jim Henson was our replacement.

Back again to channel 13, but the fire in my heart was no longer there. I didn't understand why. I wasn't even conscious of my change in attitude, and several more years had to pass before I was fully aware of what was happening in my life. Once more, in the summer of 1961, our show on channel 13 ended.

One afternoon I drove up to Fresno and, by chance, *met Cliff Ruby on the street*. His first remark was, "Bring little Webster back here, and let's get going again."

We did.

Muriel and I built a house across the street from the ninth green at Belmont Country Club.

Bobby Troupe's wife, Julie London, appeared in Fresno, and Bobby and I played a round of golf. I remember his saying, "Jimmy, the guys in Hollywood don't have it as nice as you do right here."

I bought a Mooney Mark 21 airplane and once again was scooting all over the San Joaquin Valley skies.

The years 1962, '63 and '64 emerged as perhaps the overall happiest in our lives. My old buddy, Bob Klein, was now the station manager of channel 8 in

Salinas and added Webster's show there, too.

We videotaped a show each week for Fresno's channel 47, flew to Bakersfield for a weekly taping for channel 17, and I flew to Salinas every day, doing a live show.

Who was with us? Mode O' Day and *Aunt Berniece Ruby!* Yes. She, Uncle Cliff, Webster and I were the solid *four*.

Here's that little Mooney zooming over the San Joaquin Valley. Look carefully and you'll see Webster's picture on the top of the tail.

Aunt Berniece Ruby on our commercial set, and that handsome guy in the upper left hand corner is her husband and
my dear friend, Uncle Cliff Ruby. I repeat—the most brilliant
merchandising executive I've ever known.

16. The Realization I *Had* Become a Bull Frog

One of our sponsors in Salinas was Meadow Gold Milk. The District Superintendent asked me to join him at an awards banquet for his staff—twenty-five milk men and their wives.

He had hired a special speaker, coming from San Jose, for this occasion, and wanted me to introduce him. He knew this fella had some serious things to tell his staff and hoped that some of little Webster's antics would get them in a good mood first. I was more than happy to do this, although I had no idea what impact this gentleman's speech would have on me personally.

Following Glen Lay's introduction, I went to the back of the banquet room and sat down. Within five minutes, I was straining to see what he was writing on the blackboard and listening to every word. I used all of the napkins on my table to make notes.

This is the night I first learned things which you have read throughout my book.

He printed the word *success.*

"This is the most misunderstood word in the English language. It is not a destination, but a journey that never ends. Always have a reason for getting out of bed every day!"

He then discussed the six areas of our lives that have to be dealt with on a daily basis: mental, physical, spiritual, social, family and financial. As long as we were developing our talents in these six areas, we were successful, provided we were doing what we really wanted to do. If we weren't, then we were unsuccessful.

Next, I saw the word *motivation* on the blackboard. I honestly can't remember having heard the word until that moment. Surely it was taught in high school and I was 'just not listening,' but I certainly did *that* night.

Success and motivation are synonymous with one another. The dictionary gives the definition of motivation as something which determines choice, lends direction, gives impetus to man's being. Another meaning: *a desire held in expectation with the belief that it will be realized.* Simply stated, you won't do anything on this earth you don't believe you can do. There's absolutely nothing you have ever done that you didn't first *believe* you could do.

The guy who says I *can* and the one who says I *cannot* are both right, one hundred percent of the time. Glen went on to explain that only one person out of every twenty was motivated, due to conditioning factors, which I've covered in detail.

When Conrad Hilton was a little boy seven years old, he used to sit on the floor, pretending he was a hotel operator. His parents watched his behavior and smiled at his daily performance. Then, this insatiable desire of his became a reality when he was old enough to buy what we might call a flea-bag in Cisco, Texas. He put into practice all of those things he had dreamed of doing as that little boy.

Another hotel owner was so impressed with the transformation Conrad made with his building, he visited him one day and pleaded, "Conrad, you're the best hotel operator I've ever seen in my life. Can you tell me how you do it?"

Conrad's response was not, "Heck no, get your own ideas!" but rather, "Certainly, I'll be glad to tell you what I do," and he shared all of his knowledge.

Conrad was more than happy to be of assistance, but this other fella honestly did not like the hotel business. He actually disliked it, so a few weeks later he suggested that Conrad buy him out. Conrad wasn't thinking, 'Why, I will build the biggest hotel chain in the world.' No, he just reasoned that he could extend his service to more people by having a second hotel, so he agreed, and bought it. But that *was* the beginning of the Hilton hotel chain. See the difference? Conrad loved what he was doing, while the other man was miserable.

Glen then told us how Napoleon Bonaparte used to pretend he was a general when he was a little boy, playing with toy soldiers. Please understand the importance of placing in your mind a definite goal you want to reach.

Glen said, "Don't ever stop having a reason for being. Always have something to look *forward* to... not *backwards!*

"You see, scientists will take a bull frog, just a big old frog, and drop him into a Pyrex bowl containing an inch-and-a-half of hot water. When he hits this hot water, his legs are strong and he immediately jumps out. They catch him and empty the bowl and fill it with cold water. Now they drop the frog back into the bowl of cold water which he loves. He settles down nicely, but they put the bowl over a Bunsen burner and turn the fire up a tiny bit. The frog sits there as the water slowly warms up. He doesn't move. After a while the water becomes very warm, yet he still sits there. Finally, it begins to boil, and the frog dies, never moving again. Transfer this behavior to the human mind and it is known as *complacency*. It can happen in any life... age is no factor."

Glen's words penetrated my *computer*, whirling at the speed of light. Conrad Hilton, Napoleon Bonaparte—both when they were seven years old. My experience—seeing the movie at that age. The starring role with Ronald Colman in the film ten years earlier. Suddenly, I realized I had *become that bull frog back in 1954!* Everything following that moment of personal triumph had been a succession of events *unfolding-daily-on-a-regular-road-of-life-rollercoaster.* I'd been accepting things as they developed, no longer having anything definite to work for. I had already "done it."

W hen I was a little boy, I didn't know what I was really trying to do. I knew nothing of motivation, success, or anything like that. I just planted in my *computer* what I constantly dreamed of and blindly moved forward. There was no such word as failure in my mind.

You can perceive my whole life was geared to Hollywood. Everything I did was related to show business, in some way—certainly in my *mind*. As each step on the ladder of my ultimate goal was reached, I became more confident. I didn't know why, but when I finally did achieve that one thing I had dreamed of—the movie with Ronald Colman in *Hollywood*—

my dreams ended. I had reached the summit of my mountain.

Please read the following paragraph carefully. Everything God ever created on this earth grows to a certain point and levels off. Without an infusion of new purpose and meaning, there's nothing left to do except die.

Among the bodies lying in cemeteries, there are millions whose epitaphs should read: 'Died at twenty... buried at ninety,' because those people mistook their first goal as *success* and never realized it was just the beginning. Yes, success truly is a journey that never ends. Always have something to work for, to look forward to... oh, that bull frog syndrome.

Being of service is the greatest personal reward you can get, in my opinion. Being needed by someone, being of importance to another individual, is the greatest feeling there is, which brings me to the point of your being a member of some service club in your area. There are so many and all of them are doing an outstanding work in community relations.

Our USA is a compassionate land and it shows through these organizations. To name a few alphabetically: Civitan, Kiwanis, Lions, Optimists, Rotary. I work so closely with Kiwanis Key-Clubbers, Keywanettes and Circle-Ks... young people who are the leaders of tomorrow. If you are a teenager, please become involved with a youth group sponsored by a service club. And if you are my age and have never joined one, do so and help preserve our American way of life. It's the best there is on the face of this earth, and you can be so effective... yes, *you!* (Look in that mirror again.)

Now, deeper into my personal life, you can understand the misconception I had of equating money with that of being a movie star, if you will, by wanting Bennie to become my accountant. Of course, movie personalities of international prominence earn a lot of money, and that is all I had understood as the little boy, not realizing at that age, money is such a diminutive part of it all.

I'm reminded of that young dental surgeon who despised his vocation, yet he was so very successful, in the eyes of others.

Let's search to find some solutions.

If you were to follow one hundred people starting at the age of twenty-five, you would discover each one was excited about their future. However, by the time they reach the age of sixty-five, only one will be extremely wealthy, four will be financially independent and five will still be working. Thirty-six will have died and the remaining fifty-four will be absolutely broke, depending on someone else for life's necessities. These are statistics, not Jimmy Weldon's ideas.

Yes, and Jimmy, your reference is to money, when you just said money wasn't all that important.

I know, and that's true, but we still have to earn enough money *in order to get by*. When you enjoy your work, you're so interested in doing a good job, the money automatically becomes a by-product. There's no way to stop it. Use Jonas Salk, producer of the polio vaccine, for instance. Was he struggling for money? Did he think "I've developed something that will make me rich. I'm going to charge every millionaire a thousand dollars to immunize his children. I'll be *swimming* in cash"?

No! He was developing a safeguard for mankind itself, and the money flowed in.

There's a law which guarantees whatever you *give*, you'll *receive* in return. Psychic income which never appears on an income tax report is the best compensation you can receive. Recognition from the world is far greater than the entire holdings of Donald Trump!

Here's the promise of another law: do something good for someone and they'll try desperately to pay you back. They may not be *able to* in every instance, but they'll feel the obligation. Nevertheless, that good deed *will* return from some source. For every action there is an equal and opposite reaction.

Ask any pessimist, "What will you get back when you cast your bread upon the water?"

"Soggy bread!" is his response.

But the answer I prefer is, "As ye sow, so shall ye reap." So it isn't the money. However, let's *use* money as a measuring device for now.

Why are only five out of the hundred financially independent when they reach sixty-five? All of them had dreams and optimism for the future. They believed in their own success—most of them—but something along the way caused this wide disparity in the outcomes. Here's the answer.

Goal setting and actually understanding what goal setting means really *is* the biggest difference in these individuals. I'm not speaking of some daydream fantasy—but a real concrete desire to accomplish something. That's why I said having a goal in life is the most important decision a person can make, but when it *is* attained, it's essential to set higher ones, and move forward.

L et's go back to our childhood, when we used to hear the same story over and over again. The story teller couldn't change a single word, we wanted to hear it exactly the same way every time. If they did change it, we reminded them quickly, "It didn't happen that way." And if our story teller was annoyed and said, "Then why don't you tell *me* the story," we just made a stronger demand, "No, *you* tell it, but tell it *right*." Why? because our little imaginations were wide open, ready to add more pictures to those already stored in our marvelous *computers* from hearing the story before. Each time, the story became more animated and exciting.

As a result, doctors presumed that we learn through repetition, which is absolutely absurd. *Stupid* is a better word. If this were true, we would learn all of our mistakes rather than the right things.

How? Simple. Let's use pitching horseshoes as a good example. During the learning process, a person may get only one ringer out of thirty attempts.

Excuse me. You may not be familiar with this game. The object is to pitch (toss) a horseshoe at a little iron peg stuck in the ground about twenty-feet from the spot where you're standing to pitch the horseshoe. You're trying to make the horseshoe circle the peg completely. This is called a *ringer*.

You must have heard the old saying, "close only counts in horseshoes." Well, this game is where that saying originated. If there are no ringers, then the closest horseshoe to the peg wins a point.

Remember now, I'm speaking only of the learning process. A professional horseshoe player may get four ringers out of every five horseshoes he pitches, but he couldn't do this when he started.

Now, wait. I realize he had to practice over and over to develop his skill, but we are only talking about *how he learned to do it...* nothing more.

Let's go back now. This person gets only one ringer out of the thirty times he pitches the horseshoe, when he starts learning the game.

Stop. It doesn't take any intelligence to see that he *misses twenty-nine times* if he only gets one ringer out of the thirty attempts. Therefore, if repetition is the only way to learn the game, doesn't it stand to reason that the more he practices, the better he will get at *missing*? He's practicing his misses far more than he is the *hits*. Twenty-nine to one, in fact. Can you imagine anyone saying, "Man, I'm sure getting good missing this. Yahoo!"?

No, that's <u>dumb</u>!

He keeps pitching the horseshoes and the reason he gets better is this: his *computer* is saying, 'wait... a little more to the right (or left)'... or... 'throw a little harder and it will get there'... or... 'not so much spin on the horseshoe'... uh... 'keep looking where you are throwing!' Those are the mental pictures he develops. His *computer* is making the corrections he needs to do better. He's now remembering his *hits*... not his *misses*. And he gains confidence, getting progressively better.

"Yeah, but he's still practicing," you may say. I will come right back with the same thing I said to you earlier: The person who says *I can* and the one who says *I cannot* are both right, one hundred percent of the time.

How many of our good friends have no confidence and constantly tear themselves apart reliving past mistakes and failures? Now they are afraid to make *any* decision for fear of being wrong. Oh, there are millions out there, believe me, which brings to mind the story of the young Catholic priest who had never taken confessions in a little parish. The older priest came to him one day and said, "You're going to start taking confessions today."

The young priest was happy. "Fine... huh... what do I do?"

Remember now, this is just a joke. *(tee hee)*

The older priest smiled, "Nothing. Just sit there and our parishioners will come in and give their confessions. In about thirty minutes, we'll have a little critique, and I'll let you know how you're doing."

So the young priest began hearing the confessions. With a feeling of confidence, he glanced at the older priest, who was motioning for him to stop for their discussion.

The young priest got up and said, "You all wait here, I'll be back in just a minute," (or whatever they say), and reaching the older priest, proudly expected a compliment. "How am I doing, Father?"

The reply was both complimentary and cautionary. "You're doing great, son, but I must tell you, as our parishioners are giving their confessions, just sit there and listen. You can't keep saying, 'Goll-leee!'" And I say this to you now, dear reader, stop saying golleeee about *yourself*. Your *brain* is the greatest piece of machinery that was ever created. There will never be another you.

When Glen finished speaking, I couldn't wait to ask him, "Where did you get that information?"

"It's all in the library," he calmly replied.

"You don't understand, Glen. That was *my* life you were giving."

"I wish everyone felt that way, Jimmy."

"I don't think you realize it really *was* my life you were talking about just now. Glen, I want to tell everyone I possibly can what you have just said!"

I made an appointment to meet him in San Jose. I flew over from Fresno to the San Jose airport the following three Saturdays and spent two hours each afternoon, getting all of the information I could. I worked so hard to develop a presentation, but it was impossible. I didn't have the knowledge, which was absolutely essential.

Motivation is not some mystical pillar of fire descending from heaven and surrounding us with, 'Ooooohhhh, you're motivated!' No sir. Motivation is something *you work at every day* or, like any muscle which isn't used, it will atrophy and die.

In time, I snuggled down into that little comfort zone once more where things were going all right, and my excitement on that night in 1964 slowly faded away. Until....

17. "Twee-ee Twee-ee!"

During the summer of 1969, a young fella telephoned and said, "I think I have something you will be interested in, Jimmy."

I'll never forget his marketing presentation for The Dynamics of Personal Motivation, a program produced by Success Motivation Institute in Waco, Texas. *This* was the very thing I had eagerly searched for five years earlier, but had slowly forgotten about with the passage of time.

I was so excited I could hardly stand it. The fire I had felt that night listening to Glen came back in my mind and heart. I joined SMI, enthusiastically selling this program to more husbands and wives than any single person in the organization. I held seminars twice a month for those who bought the program, and we shared the progress of our individual goals and confirmed the personal growth which was taking place. We enjoyed being together and sharing each other's ideas. It was good.

You must believe in what you are doing. Then others will, too, because they appreciate your sincerity. I truly believed this program was the best foundation for a solid family unit and had the real formula for developing love and respect husbands and wives had never experienced before.

Then it happened. Paul Meyer divorced his wife and married his secretary. My guru, the founder and president of SMI! And I was out there impregnating everyone with the confidence that this program would build an enduring love they had never dreamed of before.

I was finished!

I had no desire in the least to sell another program, but its contents were so infused as part of my life I still hungered to tell *everyone* to go after *whatever* it was they wanted!

I sincerely regard Toastmasters as the best organization there is for developing self confidence in communication—one-on-one, or speaking before a group. We're taught in Toastmasters that a good speech consists of three parts: first, tell the people what you're *going* to tell them; second, *tell* them; and third, tell them *what you have just told them*.

On the surface, that sounds a bit peculiar, but in truth, it's absolutely right. My sincere hope in writing this book was to give you information to make you aware of the fact that you *are* the most important person on Earth and, at the same time, make you realize there is no one who will ever be exactly like you—ever again—in all the world.

Man has computers doing billions of calculations per second. While one is working, all you do is pull the plug out of the electrical outlet and it stops. It has to have electrical energy to function, but *your computer* never stops. Even when you're asleep it's going full blast, and is often more productive *then* because you aren't interfering with its operation.

What are you doing with yours?

I play golf at Braemar Country Club where major

reconstruction was recently completed. They redesigned the sixteenth fairway because of a housing project. Every day, at least fifteen giant earth movers, carrying thirty tons of dirt, completely ripped away a mountain.

Now, each of the huge carry-alls had a driver sitting up in the cab, guiding it to scatter these loads of dirt at specific spots. What if each operator had started the engine and then jumped from the cab? You can quickly visualize each one lumbering along the mountain path, tumbling down the side, hurling earth everywhere, wildly spinning its wheels until it runs into something and shuts down.

Why, Jimmy, that's dumb. It certainly is, but what about you? You're reading this right now using machinery that is regarded as the greatest source of power ever made... your *brain!* Are you going to put your hands firmly on the controls to guide it carefully, providing it with good, solid positive thoughts and goals to reach for, or will you permit it to drift aimlessly in all directions from day to day?

You can program a computer to calculate two plus two equals four for years, then in a single moment reprogram it to calculate two plus two equals five. It will never pause to wonder: "What are they doing to me?" No, it will produce the new figures instantly and do whatever it's automated to do, and it can't even think! You *can.*

D id you ever stop to realize that man is the only animal that can fail? Yes. Let's examine that statement. Why does a squirrel gather nuts in the fall and put them away for the winter when it will be cold and no food will be there to gather? He was born in the spring and never experienced cold weather. How did he know it was going to *get* cold?

Next, how does a bird build a nest so intricately, yet never built one before?

Or how can the birds in the North Pole area know when to fly south to the warm areas of the earth? There are no explorer birds, no television, no newspaper or radio announcements to let them know *when* or *where* to fly, yet they fly thousands and thousands of miles over uncharted water and land right at the exact spot they need to be.

I'll be glad to tell you. Animals have a built-in success instinct, placed there by the creator.

No, God did not *shortchange* man. The one thing humans have that no other animal has is a creative imagination, and it's that special trait that makes us not only creatures, but creators as well. Using our imagination, the sky is the limit. Dream those dreams you had as a child and go after them, it's never too late. We're all children when we can *get away with it.* The only difference between an adult and a child is the *cost of the toy.* Don't ever stop being that little boy or girl you once were, because you're the same... just a little older now.

Formative years are from zero to six, doctors acknowledge. True. We learned and have kept in our *computers* all that was taught during these years of maturing. This is good, but sometimes we need to change our thinking.

Conditioning factors are extremely important. I grew up in the depression years. You never *disremember* when you were hungry or had very few clothes to wear, but our minds are capable of understanding that our *paradigms* must be analyzed now and then.

Explanation: There are so many instances of child abuse, drug addiction, perversion, and on and on and on. Our television and other media display these to the hilt. I repeat: no brothers were ever more fortunate than Bub, Moyne and I were for having such wonderful parents, so I can appreciate your feeling a bit left out, learning of my background. We often sense our own suffering as unique, but this is simply not true. We only think of it that way. Millions of others have gone through the same things you have.

You may think, "But Jimmy, there are so many terrible memories I have; so much doubt about myself. I was beat down as a child and lost all of the confidence I had. In fact, I never developed any."

Okay, I'll agree with you. How can you overcome such feelings? Take a look around. This great big old world is full of good things, and you deserve each one just as much as anyone else.

"But that doesn't help me with my memories, Jimmy."

No, but it will, when I clear up the following fact: I still believe you can reprogram your mind, unlike that computer, which is strictly fed programs created by humans.

"Yeah, but humans programmed *my* mind also, Jimmy."

Okay, here's how we'll get rid of that unwanted programmed material. Let's use a bucket brimming full of water. We're going to drop little pebbles in the bucket, and each one causes a tiny bit of water to spill over the top. We keep dropping in pebbles, and the water continues spilling over the side. After a time—*and it takes awhile*—you'll find the pebbles have replaced most of the water. This is comparable to your mind. I realize this is an over simplification, but the mind does work in this manner. Just keep feeding your *computer* good thoughts. Don't give up.

L et's examine the procedure our *computer* goes through in accepting new ideas. When we hear something that is exactly the opposite of what we think is right, we react with *total rejection*. The second time this idea is presented we move to *partial rejection*. The third exposure takes us to *partial acceptance*; the fourth time, *full acceptance*; fifth time, *partial assimilation*, and the sixth exposure brings *full assimilation*.

I'm going to explain this with an account from personal experience. Where I grew up, the mere thought of eating *snails* was one of the most stupid, ridiculous, dumb things a person could do.

Well, Muriel and I were living in Dallas in 1951 when someone mentioned they were going to have snails for dinner. I hit the ceiling. "Why the idea, anyone eating those slimy little creatures is dumb. @¤#Í¥£¢!! Dad-gum!" You can readily see, that was *total rejection*.

Months later, someone came up with the same thought, and this time, unknowingly, I'd moved to *partial rejection* when I replied, "I've heard some people eat those little critters. But not me." You see, I wasn't nearly as totally-against-it this time.

We moved to Hollywood then, and someone again

suggested a meal of snails. I calmly smiled, "Golleee, I've heard a lot of people eat those little things, but I just can't see how it would ever be something *I* would be interested in."

I had slowly been led to *partial acceptance*. (Remember, dear reader, these were just natural reactions. I didn't learn this was the way the mind works until many years later.) The fourth time I heard this idea of dining on snails made me think snails *have* to be perfectly all right; too many people think of them as a delicacy. I had progressed to *full acceptance* now.

The fifth exposure came when seven of us were dining in Musso & Frank's on Hollywood Boulevard. A guy announced he was having escargot for dinner. At long last, I had a picture of these little creatures being farmed like vegetables.

I jumped in quickly, "Hey, you're talking about snails. I want to try one when you get them."

I had moved to *partial assimilation* and did eat a little bite. I remember thinking of it as tasting something like an overcooked mushroom. Surprise! It was not totally bad at all. Mmmmmm...

About six months later, I was out in the front yard talking to a friend when he mentioned he was having snails for dinner. I told him about having had one and thinking it was pretty good. I had covered the full scope from *total rejection* to *full assimilation*. It was now *my* idea! I promise you, the things I've told you happened exactly the way I described them. Each of those exposures to the idea of eating snails had come from different individuals and over a long period of several years. Not the same person harping on an idea I disliked. In that type of situation, a mind can be permanently closed—from sheer anger itself! You know: "My mind is made up, so don't confuse me with the facts."

I'm not running up and down streets yelling for everyone to eat snails. No way! I'm merely pointing out that some things we were taught may be incorrect. Therefore, understanding that we *do* have the ability to change our thinking and behavior by studying the reasons *why* we hold feelings about some things *can* be very comforting indeed.

This thinking won't work with such stupidity as someone suggesting Joe Blow is a jerk and we ought to 'blow him away!' and after the sixth exposure to the idea, we execute him. No! That really *is* dumb!

Now, back to getting rid of that unwanted material I was talking about before the snail scenario. Feeding positive thoughts into your mind will replace old negative ones. (This is a parallel of those pebbles replacing the water in that bucket.) Oh, there will still be some deep, dark memories but you *can* get them out, just don't ever give up.

Each time a negative thought sneaks in and causes a bad attitude, replace it *immediately* with a positive belief you have in yourself, or a belief in what you are *becoming*. I repeat: You reserve the power to exercise absolute control over the most highly organized, yet incredibly complicated entity in the world. *A computer with unlimited potential. Your brain.* It will only think about what you permit it to think about. Take charge of your life!

On a three-by-five card, write the description of the person you want to be. Think about that person and begin to act like the individual you want to become. Think how you will behave when you are that person. You *will* become that person. There's no way you can *not*. That's a law just like the law of gravity. You jump off of a building and you're going to go down, not up, and it's the same with all laws. There's no exception. There will be moments when you want to give up. It just seems too difficult, but it *isn't!*

I admire Thomas Alva Edison, the man who invented the light bulb. One day after the failure of an experiment, his assistant said, "Mr. Edison, you've failed nine-hundred-and-sixty-seven times."

Edison smiled and confidently replied, "No, my good man, I've just eliminated nine-hundred-and-sixty-seven ways which won't work." Imagine, he didn't quit his inspiration, as most of us probably would have, following the second or third try, or some after the *first* attempt. No, he continued hundreds of times, roughly a thousand different experiments on the same project. He knew in his heart that he was on the right track and would not give in to failure.

Something else... Thomas Edison would often lie down and take a short nap when he was really puzzled and unable to find the answer to a problem. When he woke up, invariably he knew what he trying to figure out. Think. This is not fiction you're reading, and what Thomas Alva Edison did was not something only *he* could do. You can do the very same thing yourself. Again, I wanted to point out how our *computer* operates without interruption twenty-four hours a day, so lie down, close your eyes, focus on a problem, and then take that nap.

Edison often summoned his wife to his laboratory and asked her to please get him something to eat, and she would inform him, "You just had a sandwich and a glass of milk not fifteen minutes ago."

"Oh, all right. Thank you, sweetheart." And that was it. He didn't even remember he had eaten, he was so deep in concentration. Gollleeeeee!

Nothing is worthwhile if it is free. We need to work for what we get, but if we are excited and striving for something we really want, then what we consider work is really more play.

Wait a minute... I'm wrong in stating that nothing is worthwhile if it's free. Everything we enjoy that *is* good was given to us. Our minds, our souls, our bodies, our dreams, the love of our family. Everything that's really good *we got for nothing*, but we don't truly appreciate them.

Keep that goal before you every day. Look at it and believe in your heart you're going to become that person you really want to be, and believe you *will* be happier than you ever dreamed possible. Oh, how I wish I'd been aware of these things when I was a little boy. If only I'd understood the real reason I was so anxious to do what I'm doing. Had I known about the bull frog's predicament and finally, the importance of setting higher goals as each one is reached, my life would have been so different.

Complacency is to say "all is fine now, I'm set, *I've got it made*, I don't care about anything." Such a shame. You know people who have retired (Oh, how I *despise* that word) and have died shortly thereafter because they had nothing to live for; yet others are enjoying life, doing what they wanted to do all along, and appear younger and younger as the years roll by. What a difference.

Remember that your mind will only think about what you permit it to, and that we *become* what we think about. Many great philosophers through the ages have agreed with this concept.

Now, how does this come about? Let's use a farmer as our example. He can plant whatever he wants to. The land has nothing whatsoever to do in selecting the seeds. It will return what the farmer plants, but it doesn't have anything to say about *what* is planted.

For instance, the farmer has a seed of wheat and another of poison. He digs two holes in the ground and places a seed in each one, carefully covers them, then waters and fertilizes the soil, cultivating it properly. In time, the two seeds germinate and come up as plants. One is a healthy stalk of wheat, and the other right beside it is deadly poison. Do you realize your mind works just exactly like the land? It doesn't care what seeds you plant, but it will return anything—just like the land. They perform alike.

As a man thinketh, so is he. If you plant a concrete goal to reach, and then work for it every day, you'll surely get it—if you believe you will. Think of me, that little boy in Chickasha, Oklahoma.

Perhaps you've seen old bums lying around on the streets and wonder why they're there. *Everyone is where he really wants to be, whether he will admit this or not.* We are the sum total of our thoughts.

Oh, sure, there are those who have lost their employment, had business setbacks, illness or what-have-you, but if you follow their progress, they'll bounce back and be right on top again. A guy who is a failure continues to fail, while a person who is successful continues being successful. It's all in how he perceives himself.

You have heard it said, "Everything that guy touches turns to gold," but check the attitude of that person. You'll find it is exceptional. A man can alter his life by changing his attitude. Your attitude is the only thing you own—lock, stock and barrel. **Don't ever let anyone step on your attitude!** You can experience such happiness or sadness, all because of what someone says to you.

I always tell the wives they deserve credit for their husband's good attitude. "When your husband leaves for work (or wherever), kiss him goodbye, then yell to him, *'Go get 'em, Tiger!'* because nothing will lift his spirits higher." This is what Muriel used to call to me every time I left the house.

Twee-ee Twee-ee, which meant "I love you... twice," was written at the bottom of every note we left each other on the dining room table, or it was the ending of our air mailed letters during her *thirty-nine trips* to England. And I say to you now, if you're married, say to each other, "I love you"... at least twice a day.

In the latter part of 1962, Hanna-Barbera began producing *The Yogi Bear Show*. Every week I flew to Burbank in the little Mooney and was the voice of Yakky Doodle, the little duck. The series continued about three years. I also was the voice of Solomon Grundy on *Challenge of Super Friends* and did odd voices on other series. I still enjoy doing them.

George Tibbles gave me the encouragement I needed to start a whole *new* career I'll tell you about in the next chapter.

18. It Really *Is* 'Who You Know'...

In the winter of 1972, I spoke to four-hundred-and-fifty (salesmen and spouses) in the Mediterranean Room of the Riviera hotel in Palm Springs.

George and Mildred Tibbles were living there and joined me. Everyone was nipping the bottle and wanting to dance, so he warned, "You must speak soon, Jimmy." This was about 7:30.

8:00 — "Don't wait too late, Jimmy, for your presentation," George warned again.

8:30 — Still no one told me to speak.

8:45 — The audience was becoming restless now and rather noisy as George pleaded, "Jimmy, I've seen Don Rickles booed off of a stage similar to this, and he's an entertainer, not a speaker. These people are in no mood to hear a speaker. They have waited too late. Please don't do it!"

Just then, a gentleman stepped up to the microphone. "All right, all right. Quiet. Sit down! I have a special speaker for you tonight."

From the back of the room, out boomed the most vulgar verb and pronoun combination you can imagine. In other words, forget the speaker.

I looked at George who had buried his head on the table, along with Mil.

The voice screamed, "Listen, you (expletive), shut up and sit down. If it weren't for me, you wouldn't even be here!"

Again I looked at George, shaking his head and

looking down at the table.

The man at the microphone called, "Jimmy, Jimmy, where are you?" I was standing on the dance floor, a good five feet below the stage. He saw me as I reached up for the microphone.

I carried it to the audience area as far as it would go... about four feet from the first table. Everyone was seated in a huge semi-circle.

"I know you all would much rather dance than listen to me, but could I please just have a couple of minutes to introduce you to someone you might remember when you were little boys and girls?" (I was referring to Webster Webfoot.)

A fellow on the opposite side of the room from where the first comment had come yelled, "Let him talk!"

I waved, "Thank you, sir. Bless your heart." *Forty-five minutes later,* I turned and carried the microphone back to the stage, handing it up to the man.

When I looked back, the audience was standing. I cried, and so did George, as he hugged me.

"Jimmy, I've never seen charisma in an audience equal to this anywhere in my life. You must become a professional speaker!"

George, Mil and I slipped over to a little restaurant nearby and visited for an hour, where I penciled thoughts for our return to this area.

I became associated with an agency for speakers, and Muriel and I finalized our moving plans.

I remember her little English accent, "Oh, *Dahling,* don't make me spend another summer here in the San Joaquin Valley. It's so hot."

It does get hot up there... *Ooohhh.*

W e moved to Chatsworth, in the San Fernando
Valley, on May 20, 1973.

(Remember Mr. Campbell in Chapter 11?)

Frank Capka's been a friend since 1952. He insisted
we play golf with the one man who could launch
my speaking career.

We did, and the six foot-seven-inch giant, Bill Graham, became my buddy immediately. Bill had me
speak to the branches of United California Bank all
over the state. With his efforts, my name grew rapidly, helping me become associated with the National
Management Association, which carried my speaking engagements throughout the United States.

Bob Klein, back again. In 1973 he was marketing
director for Oakland's Central Bank and wanted us
for his branches, too. Yes, little Webster and I were
racing all over California.

I spoke to the leasing department of Central Bank,
whose division manager was George Padis. George
plays golf with John Ascuaga. I met Bill Graham on
a golf course. You meet nice people and excellent
business associates on those links.

Trust me.

You know the John Ascuaga story reported in chapter 12... the little hotel maid.

Martin Campbell, Bob Klein, Frank Capka and Bill
Graham are the ones who have reinforced my belief
in that old cliché, "It's not *what* you know, but..."

Yeah.

Nuf sed!

19. The Bombshell!

My entire book has been centered around our brain *(computer)* because it alone is responsible for success or failure. Conditioning factors from birth constantly organize most of its programming. These are inputs from friends, associates and educators, plus the hundreds of thousands of things we do every day, filling it with billions of bits of data. Combinations taken from those bits of information make up our paradigms. I could go on and on, hardly touching *the tip of the iceberg.*

I sincerely believe that any person who has the mental capacity to understand and follow the outlined instructions I'm going to go through step by step in the next chapter can accomplish anything they want to do. I have no problem with previous backgrounds, environment or what-have-you.

I said and I will repeat: Anyone capable of reading and comprehending what I will say *can* capture their ultimate dream.

Now, Jimmy... you've gone too far.

Okay, I will rephrase a portion of the statement. I'm offering my sincere beliefs to only those individuals who simply lack *personal motivation.* I exclude people with deep seated emotional scars which require professional attention because I'm not qualified in those areas; however, I will state this belief in myself: Having diligently studied the field of motivation for more than twenty-five years and related all of its aspects to personal experiences, I doubt if another human being alive knows more about this subject than your author. Secondly, I'm far more *on fire* today than I was thirty years ago when I first became *aware* of the word **motivation!**

In Chapter 11, I promised that startling *maybe-you-are-not-aware-of-facts* were coming later. Well, here they are.

Your *computer* doesn't know the difference between *real* or *imagination*. Ponder that remark and you'll want to burst out laughing. Jimmy Weldon, after all of the explanations and examples you've given in this book, you have the nerve to make that statement? Yes, I do. And for the proof, hang onto your seat for some more real eye-openers.

I don't believe there is a human being who has not, at some time or another, experienced the trauma of awakening from a frightening dream. Think of how you were perspiring. Your heart was pounding, and you were breathing so violently you were afraid you were going to die. Quickly though, you realized it was only a dream.

Okay, here's the picture. You were motionless, lying in a bed. Please tell me why on earth you woke up drenched with perspiration and with your heart pounding like you'd been running around the block? I'll gladly answer that for you, dear friend. No one had informed your *computer* that it was a dream. You see, it was giving you all of the emotions of an actual event. Furthermore, if you had the same dream night after night, you would *continue awakening* in the same manner. That's normal. It was the *dream* that set your *computer* into motion.

Now, what do you think you would do if you were hiking in the mountains and a giant grizzly bear suddenly stepped into your path? I'll answer that one, too. You would run! At the instant you *saw* the bear, all adrenalin would begin flowing through the veins to your legs, because that's the only way you have to leave the immediate area. You wouldn't stand still in awe, wondering what to do next. You'd *automatically* step into super gear.

That tiny little control center we learned about in Chapter 7 is now in charge, and you aren't actually permitted to think. Yes, it directs all of the body's stored energy to your legs and feet, shutting down every bodily function that's not needed for running. Oxygen would pour into the blood stream and lungs, and you wouldn't even have time to *think* about directing any of these actions.

Most of us learned this in high school chemistry class, but we've forgotten it. When our body is in danger, our *computer* reacts automatically, flawlessly producing all of the necessary actions for survival.

Now, that last event I told you about was a fact of reality. The first one was just a dream, yet the body's reaction was identical in each situation.

Pretty good so far, huh? Let's tackle another one.

Only one person has survived a king cobra snake bite, normally almost *instant* death for anyone. However, the man who survived was a doctor who had experimented with these reptiles for years. He had gradually immunized himself, using tiny injections of cobra venom.

Now, pretend we are in India, the home of this reptile. While we're visiting with our friends on the patio of their home, the host demands quietly, "Don't move a muscle. A giant king cobra is just five inches behind your left ear and will strike if you move the tiniest bit."

You didn't see the snake come up behind you, but those chilling words trigger instant knowledge you have of that snake, and you will likely do one of two things—either faint or die of fright, because your *computer* has communicated, "You're going to die, fella. There's no way you can escape it!"

Well now, maybe you're a bit tougher than the average individual, so I'll soften that outcome. One thing is sure. Your heart will begin pounding like a hammer, because of the sudden fear gripping your body. Beads of perspiration will pop out of your forehead immediately. Why? Once more, our *computer* doesn't know the difference between real or imagination. The host *could* be joking. Perhaps there isn't even a cobra there.... Hmmmm? How about that?

I have one more.

I remember Dad's telling us about this when I was a little boy. I didn't understand the significance of it until much later. Frank, the janitor of the First Baptist church in Chickasha, had such a wonderful outlook on life. He was always smiling and happy, so three men decided to play a prank on him.

He routinely mowed the church lawn every Monday morning. Each of the pranksters planned to pass the church in five minute intervals and ask how he felt, then mention that he just didn't look like the ol' Frank they knew so well.

It went this way:

The first gentleman called out, "Good morning, Frank."

Frank's response, "Good morning. Beautiful day, isn't it?"

Then the man walked up close to Frank and looked concerned, "Are you feeling all right?"

"Oh, yes, I feel wonderful. Why?"

"Well," he said, shaking his head and frowning, "You just don't look like your old self, Frank," and then walked on down the sidewalk, waving goodbye.

Five minutes later the second gentleman came by with the same, "Good morning, Frank, how are you today?" routine.

Frank's response was the same, but a bit slower now. "Uh, good morning. I feel great." Closer now, the number two man asked Frank if something was troubling him.

"No, I'm just fine. Thank you, though. Uh, why did you ask?"

He replied that Frank's eyes didn't reflect their old sparkle, and then he walked away.

Now, after the third man came along and presented Frank with the same statements, Frank hurried home. He was ill, but he didn't know *why!*

That was a true story. How powerful our *computer* is! It will return whatever is planted there, sometimes years later.

I'll admit that I've given you some rather far fetched examples, but always remember that the thoughts which direct a positive frame of mind can be just as powerful as negative ones.

Synopsis: Once you establish in your mind the goal you're seeking, feed your *computer* all the information you possibly can, then stop struggling to make it happen yourself.

Your brain and nervous system make up the *computer* which will provide the correct solutions. If you try to come up with the answers to your project consciously, this is the basis for nervous breakdowns, heart attacks and the need to pop tranquilizers in your mouth.

No, this doesn't mean to walk away from something. I said feed it all of the information you can. Your searching for answers and material necessary to complete an important assignment (goal) can be *fun*. Just **don't try to do it all by yourself.** You know what I mean.

I've illustrated in this chapter how your *computer* is far more capable of managing whatever you are confronted with than *you* are, but you must program it. Programming is your only assignment. Then relax and enjoy yourself. The results will appear out of nowhere.

Trivia is such a great game. Muriel and I were visiting with several friends one evening when this game first burst on the scene. Our group recalled all of the old radio shows we listened to as youngsters. We began naming the characters in each program. One fella asked, "Who was the Green Hornet's driver?" Well, we were amazed that none of us could recall his name.

Perhaps two hours later, Muriel and I were driving home when suddenly I yelled out, "Kato!"

Muriel was shocked and asked, "Oh, darling, what was that?"

I explained it was the Green Hornet's driver. I'd completely forgotten about playing Trivia, but you see, my *computer* hadn't. It was searching for the answer all of that time. I had merely relaxed and let *it* do the work, and it performed beautifully.

In Charles Darwin's book on evolution we read, "I remember the very spot in the road whilst in my carriage, when to my surprise, the solution occurred to me." He was riding in a buggy with his girlfriend. The origin of species was the last thing on earth he was thinking about, but his *computer* was developing the solution.

Can't you see now how it will do all of those things for *you*, if you'll only give it a chance?

Don't quit on me now, please.

We'll tie everything down in a single formula in the next chapter.

My sweet Ring on the set of *Anything Goes* and no, that is not me...tee hee. Yes... Bing Crosby.

20. The Formula And How It Works

How often have you asked yourself... where on earth did I leave that piece of paper with those directions? Muriel used to keep a little pad on the kitchen cabinet to write everything she needed to buy at the grocery store. A grocery list. Ever hear of one? Certainly you have. You probably make them, too. Isn't it strange how we make such good use of our *computers* to prepare grocery lists, yet we rarely assign them tasks that are important?

A definite goal

A survey of several college students, following graduation, revealed the top three percent out performed the others as much as ten to one, yet they possessed no more talent or abilities than the rest. The only difference was that the top three percent had reduced their goals to writing. There's nothing complicated in that procedure. If you think it's necessary to write the word *bread* on a piece of paper because you're afraid you might forget it the next time you go grocery shopping, then think of how much easier is it to forget something that's thousands of times more important than a loaf of bread. What could possibly be *that* urgent, Jimmy? *Your life!*

What is it you want to do? Who is that person you want to become? Write it down; look at it; think about it. You must have a defined objective, or you'll never see it happen.

Let me give you a silly *for instance.* Say you are driving down the highway and have no idea where you are headed. That's dumb, Jimmy. Well, you're right, it certainly is, but since I'm developing this scenario, stay with me. At the point you become tired or bored, I want you to pull off to the side of the road and park. OK. Turn off the ignition and look over your surroundings, because you just arrived. Where, Jimmy? I have no idea and neither would you, because you didn't know where you were going in the first place. The moment you stopped moving forward, *you reached the end of the line.*

I hope you found that bit of nonsense amusing, and at the same time consider the actual *stupidity of truth* in that make believe story. Pretty basic, huh?

Remember the little boy who was going to go to Hollywood and act in pictures? He had no idea that the *first* one would fulfill all of his dreams. He imagined how much fun it would be *forever.* Yet, unknowingly, the bull frog syndrome began the moment the director said "Action" for the first time in that picture in Hollywood, and he certainly wasn't thinking of the characteristics of a dad-gummed bull frog!

Yep. All of those bodies in cemeteries whose monuments should read, "Died at Twenty, Buried at Ninety"? Hello there, Jimmy Weldon!

Ninety-five out of every hundred people get up each morning because *everybody else does.*
"Why do you go to work?"
"Everybody else does."
They're all moving through life like a bull with a ring in its nose, acting like everyone else, absolutely

hating their job, but working. Working in order to survive. Thank goodness, they're at least striving to meet their obligations.

Why should you have a specific goal? Well, here's one excellent reason. This fellow was visiting a neighbor's wife when an automobile entered the driveway.

"Who's that?"

"That's my husband."

"Are you sure?"

"Yes, yes. I know the sound of our car."

"Where's your back door?"

"We don't have one."

"Where do you *want* one?" was his departing comment, as his body constructed a new exit.

Now, *that* is goal setting in its most descriptive manner... having something to work for!

Seriously though, it's imperative to know *where* you are headed. In order to do that, the next segment of the formula is essential.

Next: A written plan

Plan? Yes, plan. When you begin thinking of vacation time, you'll spend weeks poring over brochures, listing everything to pack, telling others what to do while you're gone, deciding the best route to take—plus a jillion *last-minute-things* to do. You review your plans again and again and become more excited looking forward to this trip. People spend a lot more time on their recreation than on improving their job skills.

Are you happy in your present situation? Many will say, "Oh, I gave up a long time ago because too many things were standing in the way of what I really wanted to do." If they would just write down every roadblock that's keeping them from doing it, they would quickly discover that the *right plan* could eliminate all of those obstacles, yet they will never realize it until they analyze it themselves.

I've stressed the urgency of writing down things to the point where you might ask, "Come on now, is it really all that meaningful?" Believe me, it is.

One day while I was eating lunch, I was thinking. If only I could make sure everyone knew I was speaking directly to them. But how? The answer suddenly came to me. "Call them by name, Jimmy, and they *have* to know you're talking to them."

Fortunately, there were only about twenty in the group. I made a seating chart and asked each one to give me their first name, and during the next fifteen minutes or so I was able to memorize every one.

They couldn't understand how I blended all of their names individually into my presentation, as though each had been the only one present. One fella was leaving for the bathroom when I yelled, "Wait a minute, Harold, where are you going? We need you!" They roared with laughter. He was so self-conscious, he turned to sit down, but I smiled and waved him to continue. However, I told him to be sure and come back, or the club would fine him, which brought more laughter from the audience.

That was more than fifteen years ago. Since then, if I have sufficient time and sit on a raised dais where I can see the entire room clearly, I can learn as many as sixty or more names. People often ask me, "How on Earth do you remember everyone, Jimmy?"

"If you had been looking at me, you would have seen how I was concentrating on that sheet of paper with all of your names. I was studying all during lunch (dinner, or whatever)." It's a shame that I have very little retention though. How I wish I had Dad's rare ability.

If someone asks me a week later, "All right, Weldon, who am I?"

"I haven't the slightest idea."

"Well, you knew everyone in the room the other night!"

"Yeah, but that was the other night, not now."

When this thought first entered my mind, I felt it really was a good addition to my presentations, but I couldn't perceive its genuine value until I had witnessed the amazing results. A person's name is so important! I can only do this by writing the names down! I could never remember *one* name, much less sixty or more, without *first* putting them on paper.

Recently, I purchased a new cassette tape program—Kevin Trudeau's Mega Memory. It's absolutely astonishing. There's no doubt in my mind that following his procedures will bring me close to what Dad was born with—instant recall. We all possess that capability, we just need to develop it. No, I'm not on his payroll. Kevin Trudeau has no idea who I am, but I urge you to develop your *computer* to its highest proficiency.

I've heard many speakers make this statement: "I want to speak before the audience is tired and bored." Not me! I ask the program chairman to let me be the last thing on the agenda. The more I hear, the more I can build into my presentation, and the audience realizes it's not a memorized speech.

Now, back to the reason for writing *your* plan to determine each step you take. Can you accept my belief that without a written plan your goals will be as impossible to achieve as making a good picture out of a bad negative? Oh yes, this is a good comparison. If you don't know precisely what you are after, your goal may be as much as fifty to sixty percent out of focus when you've reached it. I accomplished all I had dreamed of as a little boy when I made the motion picture with Ronald Colman. How pathetic? In reality, it was only the *beginning!*

I think this next story will be the clincher to verify the value of writing down specific things to do.

Ivy Lee, an efficiency expert, made an appointment with Andrew Carnegie, president of Bethlehem Steel. Ivy Lee wanted to submit a plan of innovative ideas to improve the production of their company.

Andrew Carnegie told Ivy Lee that they already knew *what* to do, but if he could come up with a plan to show him *how* to do what they *already knew* to do more efficiently, then he was interested.

When he heard this, Ivy Lee said, "That's the easiest part of all." He had Andrew Carnegie write down the five most important things to accomplish the following day, which took only a few minutes.

Then Ivy Lee instructed Mr. Carnegie to rewrite those five things in order of priority. In other words, place the most important item he had to do at the top of the list, the second most important in number two position, and so on. Again, this took a very short time.

The next instruction was the most critical of all.

"Mr. Carnegie, tomorrow morning when you come into this office, begin working on that list of things you've written in the exact order.

When you've completed it, start another list with five items. You'll discover you have accomplished more by two o'clock than you perhaps have done in the past month. Then, after you see its effectiveness, give this method to your plant managers to implement throughout the plant."

Andrew Carnegie asked Ivy Lee what his fee was for having provided this *service* and he replied, "Oh, after you see what it does, just send me whatever you feel it's worth." The whole interview lasted less than ten minutes, yet in a few weeks Ivy Lee received a twenty-five thousand dollar check in the mail.

Dear reader, this happened long before your parents were even born, which means in today's economy, that check would translate into hundreds of thousands of dollars. It brought Bethlehem Steel from the position of a small company to a major corporation—all by writing down a list of five things to do, doing them in sequence, and then making a new list when that one was finished.

And we use our *computers* to make grocery lists. DAD-GUMMMMMM!

Nuf sed!

Before closing this segment, let's sort of *capsulize* the notion of knowing *where* you're going and *how* to get there.

I want you to imagine standing on the ground in an area that is completely flat. Naturally, you have unrestricted visibility in all directions. A lone tree is standing one hundred feet above the horizon approximately a mile away. The air is crisp. A thin cover of fine, powdered snow provides an illusion of endless space, highlighting the silhouette of that tree. A cloudless blue sky above and nothing but white silky snow at your feet is the complete setting.

Now, the only thing I want you to do is walk directly to that tree.

Hey, what an easy assignment. Yes!

You begin walking, and after about fifty steps, I make a slight alteration in the procedure. I want you to change your direction of sight. Yes, you merely are required to look down—right in front of your feet. Why, that shouldn't present a problem, so you just bend your head down and continue your stride.

Here is a strange thing. In a surprisingly short time, you will cross your own tracks in the snow. Since you have no direction indicator other than your balance, you unconsciously start walking in huge circles. You can see it's virtually impossible to get to the tree, unless I let you look at it.

I give you that permission. You locate it and keep your eyes on that tree. There is no instrument on the market that could guide your path more accurately. You proceed to the goal... that tree. Simple?

Yes, and that imaginary goal would be no easier to reach than a real one, if you had the *plan* to guide your every step.

Should you run into interruptions from well meaning family members or associates offering all sorts of suggestions, you hold up the paper and announce, "Look, I am already on my way. I know where I'm going. It's *all* written down... right *here*."

Third: An Intense Desire

I've stressed repeatedly that you can do *anything* you really want to, if you believe you can. Your *desire* to accomplish something is equally important, yet it is often overlooked. Desire is the catalyst to goal setting. Without an intense desire to bring to an end what it is you have determined for yourself, you'll never do it.

I want you to visualize a picnic area now. Hot charcoal squares fill the bar-be-cue pit. Steaks are sizzling on the grill, and baked potatoes, wrapped in aluminum foil opened at the center, have creamy butter melting through the halves. Picture tasty, crunchy, garlic bread; the aroma of Boston-baked beans in a big pot... and fresh, percolating coffee that's sending waves of mountain grown flavor to your nostrils.

Think!

You not only *smell* this delicious treat, you can *taste* it as well. Your saliva glands are causing your mouth to water because your *computer* doesn't know the difference between real or imagination, and it's filling you with the real sensations you read about just now. If not, go back and re-read it slowly; really concentrate on that scene. I'll wait.

Mmmmmmmmm. Wow! See?

You must develop that same intense desire to reach the goal you have set for yourself. Imagine yourself doing what it is you *will* be doing when you're there. Visualize it so vividly that you are genuinely convinced this is what you desire more than anything! Work will then become play, as you strive for that goal, because you *can feel what it will mean to you when it's yours.*

We are all motivated by end results, not by methods. I graphically point this out to students with this 'for instance'. I place the setting as an area about fifty feet long, ten feet wide and a foot deep, filled with mud.

Now, someone strolls by wearing their finest clothes, and I suggest they walk through the mud. Their reward will be a brand new one dollar bill when they step out on the other side. What a ridiculous suggestion! No sensible person would consider such a thing.

However, if sitting on the other side of that mud was a brand new thirty thousand dollar Corvette and I said it was their gift the moment they reached it, there would be no hesitation at all. They would dive in, crawling through that mud. "Golleeee, I can bathe tomorrow!" would be their attitude.

You can easily perceive *that* goal would be worth far more than the trouble it would take to reach it.

Then you must be absolutely convinced that whatever it is you desire is as crystal-clear as the muddy area I just described, and that when you have achieved your goal, it will be worth all of the effort necessary to get it.

Next comes the one ingredient that your *computer* generates itself.

Fourth: Extreme confidence!

Without the proper *knowledge*, there's no way to develop confidence in yourself to accomplish what it is you desire.

Several years ago in a class room, I told a junior high school student, "You'll be a much better football player when your grades are the best they can be, because the education your *computer* is receiving now is the most valuable asset you'll have later in life!"

You can acquire knowledge about anything. The libraries are full of whatever it is you're seeking. I heard a fella state, "In five years you can become an expert on anything," and fleas were his example.

We all laughed, but he pointed out the fact that there are so many flea species in the world you would never believe it until you verified the numbers.

He went on to state, "If you were to study all of them—learn the habits, everything about *every* flea family on the earth—it would require circling the globe to gather the facts from different authors and scientists in each particular area.

"Delving into the smallest detail, you would become more knowledgeable than the authors themselves, because each would only know about the fleas he (or she) studied, but *you* would know them all.

"Your reputation as a flea expert would expand so rapidly people would say, "Ask 'so-an-so,' he's the authority on fleas."

Now, I realize that's a silly example, but think about the literal truth in what this means. My brother, Moyne, is right. No one has cornered the market on brains. You can acquire the knowledge necessary to accomplish whatever it is you're striving for, and this is where *confidence* enters the overall design.

Nothing will lift you up higher or hold you up longer than the faith and confidence you have in yourself and your abilities, and *that* comes through knowledge alone... nothing else.

Last: Determination!

This segment of the formula is the equivalent of placing the lid on a boiling pot. Whatever it is you really want to do, you must have the determination to continue... regardless of what others say, think, or do. It is impossible for anyone to gather all of the knowledge *you* have and come up with your same evaluations.

Now, this doesn't mean you should stop seeking advice now and then. What I am suggesting is, don't let anyone discourage or convince you to change your intended goal.

The desire to do what *you* want can never be experienced by another human. There'll never be another person exactly like you.

You are absolutely *one-of-a-kind*.

Charles Kettering was explaining this to a friend by stating, "What you tell yourself is so important, and the mind can do whatever you want it to, if you think about it."

His friend, Joe, was unimpressed, so Charles figured out a method that would provide unquestionable proof. He bet Joe that if he hung a bird cage in the foyer of Joe's home, Joe would put a bird in it. Joe immediately accepted the wager because there was no doubt whatsoever that he would leave the cage empty.

Charles Kettering bought this beautiful bird cage and hung it in the entryway of Joe's home.

Everyone who came in asked, "Joe, where's your bird?"

"I don't have a bird," he would quietly admit.

"That's dumb, Joe."

A little boy visiting, "Oh, what a beautiful bird cage. Did the cat eat your bird, Mister?"

"Uh, I don't have a bird," was Joe's nervous answer.

"You mean you have a bird cage without a bird in it? That's dumb!" even the lad reasoned.

Several weeks later, Kettering paid Joe a visit, and a beautiful bird was sitting in the cage.

"Oh, I see you have a bird, Joe," Kettering observed smiling.

"Yeah, I got a bird."

"Why did you buy it, Joe?"

"I got tired of telling everybody why I didn't have one!" Joe was glad to pay Kettering the money for his bet.

You see, when you sincerely plant anything in your *computer*, it automatically becomes a *verbal* bird cage, and you won't rest until it is filled!

I remember so vividly the other paper boys laughing at my attempts to imitate R.M. John while we were folding our newspapers, and Thomas Edison's assistant reminding him of the repeated failures.

If your determination is strong enough, nothing will discourage you.

No one can see in your *computer* to discover what you know, and things are not always as they appear to others.

This Catholic nun was driving her little Volkswagen across Texas on a hot summer day when she ran out of gas. She remembered having passed a service station a mile earlier, so she walked back for some gasoline. *(Yes, this is another joke.)*

She told the attendant, "Sir, my Volkswagen is out of gas about a mile up the road. Would you please give me some gasoline in a container which I'll return as quickly as possible?"

He regretfully replied, "Sister, we don't have any containers."

"Oh, it's so hot out there, and I'm in a terrible hurry," the nun painfully pleaded.

"I'm sorry, Sister. I can't close the station. I'm alone. You'll just have to wait until someone comes along who carries a gas can in their car."

Trying to find a solution some way or the other she suggested, "Would you look again, please?"

"For what?"

"Maybe you have a container you're not aware of," the Sister meekly offered.

"I know what's in my station, Sister, but I'll look anyway."

He started searching and, waaaay back upstairs, he found an old fashioned bedpan.

He smiled, shaking his head, "Why, I didn't even know this was up there, Sister."

She happily exclaimed, "All right! Blow out the dust and give me some gas."

He did.

She toted the bedpan back to her little car and, while carefully emptying the gasoline into the tank, a big truck passed carrying two men.

The driver's *paradigm* instantly made a decision. "Tom, look at that. That's the greatest act of faith I ever saw in my life!"

What they *thought they saw*, really wasn't.

W ebster and I appeared for the Western Society of Dental Surgeons in Ontario, Canada in 1976 at the Banff Springs Hotel. I watched with extreme interest the presentation of an outstanding service award. The recipient was a dental assistant who had remained in the same office for twenty-seven years.

Following the evening's festivities, I approached her, "Please tell me about your life."

She smiled, "Jimmy, I have to be one of the most fortunate people on Earth. I love my work. I have a wonderful husband. We have a great family. Our social life couldn't be better, and our lives are wrapped around our church."

She truly validates the following statement: When you reach the point in life where productive work is a reward, in and of itself, you'll never have another motivational problem. You just rework that formula over and over again.

Dear friend, it has been a wonderful experience, penning these beliefs for you in my book, and I'll repeat if I may. It's not what you *say* to people that counts, it's what they *believe* of what you say that really matters.

The following chapter will reveal your author... from another perspective.

21. The Real Jimmy Weldon

People often ask me, "Are you always as happy and full of life as you seem to be?" It's virtually impossible to feel great every day. No one is immune to sadness, and with man's cynicism anyway, you receive bad vibes from people constantly.

Have you ever walked into an office feeling great, and happily greeted the person behind a desk with a broad smile and bright, "Good morning," only to be shocked by, "Yeah, *what's good* about it?"

You felt like yelling back, "I don't know, I just thought I'd throw that out at you!"

Turn on the television. What do you see? Bad news! They'll promote anything that's totally negative in nature. Check the daytime television shows. All of the guests on these programs are oddball characters promoting some sort of lifestyle totally foreign to normal behavior, yet they're there to be seen.

Nuf sed!

A-n-y-w-a-y, back to The Real Jimmy Weldon. People act the way they think people *think* they should act. We all do.

Re-read that statement. It can be confusing; however, it is correct. For instance, Mr. and Mrs. Smith have a little girl named Bonnie. She's about five years old, and in the presence of her mother, she hears nothing but condemnations, "I don't know what I'm going to do with you. You go from bad to worse. You're just a little devil."

Her father's affirmations are just the opposite. "I love you. You're the apple of daddy's eye. You're the sweetest little girl in the whole world, and I'm so proud of you."

Well, let someone visit the Smiths for a while. That person will see little Bonnie has both good and bad traits, like everyone else. However, if that person is really an astute observer, they'll see a strange thing. In the presence of her mother, she *is* the little devil her mother expects her to be, and when she's with her dad, she's the little angel he *tells* her she is. Yes, we do act like we think others think we should act.

I answered the telephone in my office one morning with my regular greeting, preferably on the first ring, and heard, "Jimmy Weldon, this is Jeff Nicholas in Hanford. I have on my calendar, call Jimmy Weldon and feel good today."

I cried. I was so honored to think he wanted to call me, because I might make him feel good. You see, if I answer the telephone like any normal person, the caller thinks, "Uh oh, what's wrong with Jimmy?" Yes, that's right. I can't say *hello*... I have to yell out, "Hello there, sorry to keep you waiting, what may I do for you?" or something equally as nutty.

I had an 8 a.m. interview at the Warner Brothers Studio. The director asked how I felt and heard my usual reply, "If I felt any better, I couldn't stand it."

Later, my agent was laughing when I answered the phone. I asked him what was so funny and he said, "Jimmy, that director called and asked me, 'What in the hell was that guy *on* anyway? He burst in here at 8 o'clock and came back with this *if I felt any better I couldn't stand it* routine when I asked how he was feeling'."

I confessed to my agent then, "I thought I had a funny reaction when I said it this morning."

He continued, "I told him you were on the best thing that could be found, and if he were to call you at two in the morning, he'd hear the same thing!"

One morning early this year, probably in March, I was sitting here at the computer making notes for a speaking engagement I had in a few days, when it dawned on me to check how many books I had left. I began with 10,675 in 1990. They've never been for sale in stores; just people buying them from me at personal appearances or ordering them for friends and relatives, and those I've given to others.

When I saw there were less than four hundred books left, I knew I should order some more. Then I began thinking. I have this new computer with a built-in thesaurus. Why not rewrite the book using better words? Maybe making it more interesting? Yeah! I really got excited and *jumped in with both feet.*

I was going to bed at two or three in the morning, day after day. If I wasn't speaking or flying somewhere, I was sitting here pecking away, having the time of my life—just like a little kid again.

After about two months, I thought it might be a good idea to let some friends read what "the new Jimmy Weldon" had written so far and report their evaluations. My Apple IINT laser printer was shuffling out pages like it was a regular PIP center down the street. I mailed them to my carefully selected buddies, asking each one to read the material and pretend it came from someone they did not know.

I wanted their honest opinion. I wanted to know if they felt it was worth having printed.

What an error *that* was! Each one returned the same verdict: "Jimmy, you lost it. You lost it all!"

I lost what? The Jimmy Weldon *way of talking*. I spent hours on the telephone, by cassette tape, and in person, explaining to those friends that I had done *exactly what I had intended to do in the first place.*

K en Marchant, a real good buddy and excellent professional writer, did make a suggestion that I accepted immediately. "Change all the chapter titles to build curiosity in anyone who picks up your book from the shelf, Jimmy." Heck, that was the last thing I would have *ever* thought of doing. Originally, the first chapter was titled How It All Started, and I admit, that doesn't do a whole lot for anyone.

In fact, Ken asked me, "How would you feel if you looked at a contents page and saw the title, How It All Started? What is this "it" that all started?" I could see his point at once.

He continued, "Jimmy, the opening words in your book are so powerful... Mama, he killed that little girl!"

I laughingly answered, "Well, should that first chapter be titled *The Witnessed Murder?*"

"Yes! Yes! Can't you see how that ties in with those opening lines?"

"But Ken, it wasn't a murder."

"No, but you certainly *thought it was* when you were telling your mother, Jimmy."

"Yeah, but won't people think I've deceived them by—"

"No, Jimmy," Ken quickly came back, "No one will object. You were only telling the truth, and this is a writer's way of presenting a story that does make it more entertaining and exciting. What do you think you should do, start off by saying, Now, I'm going to tell you that I thought there was a murder, but don't worry, it was only—"

"Okay, okay, Ken. I understand. I understand," and I renamed all of the chapter titles you see.

Bill Mitchell produced little Webster's show on channel 13 after we came back from New York. He later wrote *The Dating Game*, *The Newlyweds*, *Press Your Luck*, *Who Done It*, and several other shows. I was talking to him on the phone, asking his advice about my new project.

He liked the idea of the title changes at once. As I was reading them he said, "Excellent, Jimmy, excellent!" I mentioned that I wanted to delete much of the material that was not motivational in the book.

"Why, Jimmy?"

"Well, for instance, on the fifth page I say, 'You may have gotten this book from me personally, after hearing me speak somewhere. So many people had asked if I'd ever written one, it finally registered that maybe I should do it.'"

"What's wrong with that, Jimmy?"

"Bill, who cares about my telling how I decided— uh—well, say *you* lived in Florida, and never heard of Jimmy Weldon, and read what I just said. What would *you* think?"

"I'd want to hear you speak somewhere."

"Aw, Bill, come on."

"Jimmy, listen. I'm not sure you should change the way you wrote your book."

"Bill, let me read you the first page. You have the original version, so you can compare it with my new way of telling it. I'm not changing any of the facts, only the way they were told. Nothing else.

"Okay, Jimmy. Let me hear the first page." I proudly began.

Chapter One
The Witnessed Murder

"Mama, he killed that little girl."

"What little girl?"

"Mama, I saw him. *He killed her!*"

"Babe, what in the world are you talking about?"

A little seven year old boy, frightened and confused, was struggling to verbalize his trauma. She knelt down tenderly wrapping her arms around him. With a selection of carefully defined child-like graphics, she removed this terrifying photograph as skillfully as a surgeon extracts a bullet. A brilliantly woven tapestry of unlimited possibilities was substituted in his fertile imagination.

"**Jimmy! You're too pontifical!**"

I was stunned. "I'm what?"

"Never mind. Are you trying to write a text book?"

"Heck no, Bill. I just thought—"

"Well, forget it. And order some more of your books, just the way they are."

"Uh, thank you, very large! I love ya, guy."

"Same here, and Webster, too. Oh, by the way, Jimmy, that line on the fifth page of your book which states: 'and you are the only person you are never going to leave' is so powerful... and true; and I think it should be in bold print."

Thanks to Bill Mitchell, it *is* now.

Following that conversation, my *computer* began to debate with me, making me realize I was not meeting a resistance from my friends because of their preconceived *paradigms* of Jimmy Weldon.

"Let's weigh the evidence," was my *computer's* first suggestion. "Are you a professional watchmaker who, for hundreds of years, built watches, and then turned down the new concept of quartz watches?"

"Certainly not! That's dumb!" was my immediate response.

"Okay," my *computer* continued, "Is it not true that your English teacher told your own mother you were the very last one to turn in your book reports, but that you remembered more about them than any other student?"

"Yes, but what does that have to do with—"

"Hold it!" my *computer* demanded, "I'm the interrogator here. You must remember, you didn't like to read *then*, and you *still* don't like to read today. In fact, you seldom read anything that does not pertain to flying."

"But... uh... after all... I'm seventy-one years of age," I tried to reason.

Now, most brazenly, my *computer* snapped back, "I'll become *you* now and say as *you* would, don't give me that stuff, fella. You tell everyone never to retire—always have a reason for—"

Wham! I was no longer meek and apologetic, because my *computer* had struck a nerve with that assertion. I shouted, "Wait a minute. Wait—just—

one—minute! I wasn't referring to retirement, I just meant that it is a bit late for me to start *reading* at seventy-one years of age."

I felt a peacefulness as my *computer* announced softly, "Now we're in agreement, Jimmy. Follow the advice of your friends. Throw away that new fangled thesaurus and tell your story just as before. You have new ideas to incorporate. Fine. But nothing *has* changed. It's four years later, that's all."

"Uh... thank you, *me*."

Dear friend, sometimes *visiting with yourself* is not all that bad.

Now back to this chapter... The Real J.W.

D ad suffered a slight stroke sometime in 1968, others in the next few years, and then additional problems involving a declining heart became evident, but he *hung in there*, struggling hard to preserve his great attitude... which he did!

On April 30, 1971, about two in the morning, Bub called. (Muriel and I were living in Fresno then.)

"Verne, this is Bub. Daddy's gone."

"What?" I screamed back.

"Yeah, we just got the call from the hospital." (Dad had been there for only a day or two.)

"Where's Mama?"

She came to the telephone. "Babe—"

I quickly cut her off with, "Dad-gummit, he's done it again."

"What, Babe?"

"He beat us there!" was my quick response.

I promised Mom I would see her shortly and I drove down later that morning.

At Dad's funeral, sitting next to Moyne, I found myself grinning silently as I looked at the casket, listening to the minister. He didn't know Dad like one of *us*, and I decided right then what I really wanted to do.

Later, in the living room of Mom and Dad's mobile home, I startled everyone, "Mom, if God lets me live longer than you, would you allow me to preach your funeral?" Well, before they all recovered from that initial shock, I continued, "And how would you like to know what I'll say, before you're gone?" That made it almost a joke.

Mom smiled, "All right, Babe."

"I'm going to step in the pulpit and announce, 'I promise you one thing, you're going to feel a whole lot better when you walk out of here than you did when you came in.'"

The family then had an honest discussion of truth about how it was impossible for a minister to know what a close relative does, but what relative could possibly do this? I assured everyone I could.

Muriel was the epitome of health and sunshine. She was never sick. Never! She had been on the television series, *Little House on the Prairie*, from its very beginning—for eight years—never missed a single day's shooting. Now she was seen as a regular nurse on the *Trapper John* series, and enjoying life so very much. Everyone called her "Mrs. Happy."

However, she hadn't been feeling well beginning about the middle of May 1987. Our regular doctor was on vacation, so we went to another who suggested a colonoscopy. He then sent us to a surgeon who requested one more test.

On the morning of June 18, I had scored the front nine holes in even par at Braemar Country Club. Muriel left word to call her at the little snack bar where we have our lunch.

I did, and she informed me, "Darling, the doctor wants me to be in the hospital at noon."

"I'll meet you there, Sweetheart."

I said goodbye to the fellas, and that was the last game of golf I was to play for almost a year. Muriel's operation was the following morning, and her surgeon had requested that I meet him afterwards in the hallway near the entrance.

I shall never forget the complete feeling of utter hopelessness when he calmly declared, "Mr. Weldon, your wife has terminal cancer."

I could struggle forever to describe the following moments, which seemed an eternity, but there's no possible way on Earth to do it. I promise you, nothing can be more absolutely devastating than hearing this about your *mate*.

Muriel was unaware she had terminal cancer. Wait, let me retract that to some extent. She was told by every doctor that some cancer remained in the colon area, but there was a good fifty-fifty chance that chemotherapy would take care of it.

If only I had been given that hope as well. The surgeon who operated on her was definite in his statement. It was terminal!

Mom was present when the surgeon's assistant again confirmed her illness was definitely terminal, but he would not predict any length of time she would live.

"Make every day count, that's all I can say." We never revealed to Muriel what either doctor disclosed.

She recovered completely (by her appearance) and returned to the *Trapper John* television series, but as time passed, there were tests... tests... tests. We spent the next eight months constantly in and out of hospitals. I state sincerely that the Screen Actors Guild is the greatest union in this United States. Special arrangements for Muriel paid all of her bills, or it would have required everything we had in the world.

I drove the freeways daily crying my heart out, plunging from 187 to 145 pounds. Mom would often say, "Ring, I'm sure I'm going to have the same thing you have one day."

I pleaded with her not to keep saying that, but she continued. On about September 15th, 1987, Mom had an operation. Cancer of the colon, exactly like Muriel.

During the following months, I'd often hear, "Oh, I hope Mommy doesn't have to suffer as I have." I'd rub Muriel's back night after night with Ben Gay or whatever could soothe her soreness and pain.

Bless her heart, she never really and truly complained, but I died slowly along with her, wishing it were my body being tortured rather than hers.

In retrospect, I wish so much we had never elected to undergo chemotherapy. We understood nothing of its potential destruction. The nurse actually confessed the last two treatments were more harmful than helpful. Without that medication, her little body could have done more fighting, I think. However, this is my personal opinion.

March 5, 1988, a Saturday morning, I was sitting by her bedside, crying my heart out, when she begged,

"Darling, please pray to let Jesus take me now."

"Ring, what's going to happen to *me*?"

She smiled, "Oh, sweetheart, you have such a wonderful life motivating others about their future. Don't cry. *I'll just be there waiting for you.*"

The nurse gave her a shot. I asked what it was, and she only advised it was the doctor's orders.

Muriel smiled, "It's all right, Darling, everything's going to be just fine."

I still wonder what was in that syringe, because shortly after its injection, she closed her eyes and went to sleep. I never was able to awaken her again. She slipped off of this ol' earth at three minutes past four that afternoon.

Her closest friend from England, Paddy Jover, had immigrated to America after World War II also, and was with me at this moment. She was one of the Four Pairs, in the show at the Coliseum that I wrote about in a previous chapter.

I have a book, written by a surgeon who states, "There's no such thing as false hope. Many doctors tell their patients that 'nine out of ten people die of this disease,' but I tell my patients, 'You're that tenth person'." He believes many people are walking the streets today because he *said* they were going to live. How I thoroughly agree with that man. The mind is so powerful. So powerful!

Robert Donner and I have known one another since *Funny Boners*, in 1955. He came to the house the day before Muriel's memorial service, hugged me and smiled, "Weldon, I just came by to tell you we all loved Muriel, but you're such a nut, we've had to put up with you, just because of her." I thanked him and he continued, "No, I know why you're as strong as you are. Some guys lose their wives and cry and wail and want everyone to see how sad they *look*, but they couldn't care less about having lost them. You, on the other hand, really did love Muriel, and you know where she is, and you'll see her again."

I gave Muriel's memorial service. Everyone discouraged me, "You can't do this, Jimmy," but my answer was firm, "I'm the only one who can!"

When I walked in the sanctuary, Denver Pyle and his wife were seated at one side, and I slipped over and leaned down, "Denver, why are you and Tippy sitting way over here at the edge?"

Smiling, he replied emphatically, "Weldon, if the show's no good, I'm leaving."

Now, not for Mom, as I had planned to do one day, but for Muriel, at exactly three o'clock, I stepped into the pulpit and opened with, "I promise you one thing, you're going to feel a whole lot better when you walk out of here than you did when you came in." And at 3:27, the little alarm on my watch rang, and I began to close. The service ended at exactly 3:30, and we all went upstairs in the Fellowship Hall and had coffee and cookies.

Most of those attending this memorial service were *her* friends in the Screen Extras Guild, many with whom I had spoken on the telephone, but never seen until that day.

They did love Muriel.

Later, I received the new Extras+Plus book, which was published by Harris Weingart, Muriel's commercial agent. Her picture was in the centerfold.

In Memory of Muriel Weldon.

My darling "Ring" — the page in Harris' EXTRAS+PLUS

Boy, that one knocked me out!

Since that service, I end all of my presentations with prayer. Everyone holding hands.

One morning, a group of high school students, seven-hundred-and-fifty sitting in the gymnasium, were holding hands, as we ended the program. The principal squeezed my hand and whispered, "Jimmy, we can't do this, but you can. God bless you!"

The only time my action was ever questioned was at Burbank High School, which required two assemblies for the entire student body. Following the first one, I was chastised by the student body president for having closed with prayer and forced to promise it would not be repeated. I felt as though I had perhaps innocently omitted the most important segment of that second assembly.

Mom duplicated Ring's course. After the doctor determined he had helped all he could, he didn't recommend chemotherapy. It would have been so severe on her body, killing the good cells as well as cancerous ones. Aware she really didn't have that much longer to live, the doctor thought it best not to suggest that medication.

On January 6th about 11:30 at night, I was sitting next to her, as she started singing *Amazing Grace*. I squeezed her hand, "Oh, yes, Mom. Yes! When we've been there ten thousand years, bright shining as the sun, we've no less days to sing God's praise than when we first begun."

About twenty-six hours later—January 8, 1989 at 1:26 in the morning—Mom breathed a big sigh while I was holding her hand.

She had requested a closed casket and just a graveside service. Mom's body was placed next to Dad's, and I reminded those present that I had asked way back in 1971 to speak at her funeral.

Suddenly a thought dawned on me. My dearest friend in show business, Dick Haynes, and his wife, Bobbie, then my beloved Muriel, and now my sweet Mom. I was left here all alone out of our special little group. Many of you find yourselves with the same terribly lonesome, almost unbearable sense of desperation and want to scream out.

"God, why? Why?"

I've stated many times, "One day, I'm going to ask Him why He did this." But by then, I'll have all the answers, and won't need to ask.

So don't fuss at yourself for having similar feelings at times. It's only because we're human that we feel this way. He understands, I'm sure!

Sometime in the early part of 1989, I had a call from Ken Hiatt, a great friend whom I had known for about twenty-eight years.

"Jimmy, I have cancer of the colon."

Oh! Another one!

I watched Ken slowly die, after months of the greatest fight on Earth. He was in St. Joseph's Hospital, right where Muriel had stayed, the fourth floor of the south wing. It's simply referred to as Four South... terminally ill patients.

We had prayer meetings in his room. All of his family was there. We cried, laughed and talked about our *future* together. He said goodbye on October 30th, and was buried the following Thursday morning. I was privileged to say a few words at his funeral, too.

I realize the sign on my wall states: 'Jimmy, you are a motivator, not a preacher,...' but, in my heart, I sincerely want to say that Father Time marches on. Those of you reading this will someday be summoned to leave here, also. Where will you spend eternity?

I love the story of the little boy who entered the drug store and asked, "Mr. Brown, may I use your phone?"

"Sure, Johnny."

He walked over and dialed a number.

"Hello, I'd like to apply for a job as a gardener.

"Oh, you've got a gardener?

"Is he a *good* gardener?

"Are you sure you're perfectly satisfied?

"You don't want to make a change?

"Well, thank you anyway." He hung up and started out the door.

Mr. Brown called, "Stay in there, son, I'm proud of you. Don't you give up, and you'll get a job as a gardener."

Johnny turned around smiling, "Who's looking for a job as a gardener? Not *me*, Mr. Brown."

"Son, don't lie to me, I heard you ask that person on the phone just now for a job as a gardener."

"No," came back his happy response, "It's this way, I *am* their gardener. I was just calling to check on myself to see how well I'm doing."

Don't ask anyone else, ask yourself. How well are *you* doing right now? That day *is* coming.

22. Jack Webb... Whatta Guy!

I wanted to do one more part as an actor before leaving Los Angeles in 1956.

I met Herm Saunders, Jack Webb's producer, and played a role in *Dragnet*. I was so thankful I had memorized my script, and you'll understand why shortly.

As I entered Mark VII productions, Jack was passing by. He paused, said nothing, lit a cigarette... all the while, looking straight at me. He then walked onto the set. I heard him say, "Let's go," and watched him walk over to a man standing behind a counter.

He said quietly, "At the beginning of this scene, I'm going to narrate over thirty seconds of silent footage, so at the signal, I'll go right into our dialogue. Do you understand?"

"Yes, sir," the fella replied confidently.

"All right. Roll it," Jack ordered.

The assistant said, "It's rolling, Mr. Webb."

Jack looked at this man and said something to the effect, "Just look at me as though we're talking. As I told you, my narration will be over this part of the scene. You understand, don't you?"

"Uh... uh, yes, sir, I think so," he replied, a bit unsure this time.

"Good."

Jack complimented the man's appearance, and also gave the wardrobe department an equal share, for selecting his clothes for the scene. The guy smiled and thanked him. They just sort of talked about the weather... anything. However, the instant the assistant director called out, "Thirty seconds," Jack changed into character and never missed a beat, "How'd you know he was dead?" The man just stood there, he was so shocked that Jack's line came with no pause at all.

Jack said, "Cut!"

Then, turning to the man, he reminded him to please keep concentrating, so they could get it done.

The actor looked embarrassed and apologized. Again, the camera rolled, and the thirty seconds cue was announced.

"How'd you know he was dead?"

This time he did respond, "Well, it was obvious he was dead."

"How is that?" was Jack's next question.

"Obviously he was, because...."

Jack was a bit more perturbed now, "Cut! How many 'obviouses' do you have in this script?"

The guy stammered and said, "Uh... uh, I... uh, well, I know those two are there, and, uh...."

"Don't say but one 'obvious'—wherever you want to put it. Roll the camera, let's get this done."

Once more, following the thirty seconds cue, "How'd you know he was dead?"

The man nearly fainted he was so nervous, but managed to come out with the line, "Well, it was obvious he was dead."

Again, Jack asked, "How is that?"

The poor guy said, "Obviously," and paused as he stammered, "Oh, there's that 'obvious' again!"

Yelling out loud now, Jack said, "Keep it rolling,

we're going to try this one more time. How'd you know he was dead?"

The man was so flustered he had no idea where he was, or if there had *been* a dead body, other than his *own*, by this time. He just stood there.

Jack walked away shaking his head, "Read the lines to another camera. We'll pick up our lines later," and proceeded to the next set. The one I was to be in!

I heard this loud, "Sheldon... Jimmy Sheldon!" and I roared back, "It's Weldon." And then I spelled it out, "W-E-L-D-O-N!"

I was going out of there *swinging*, at the very least.

Ben Alexander entered first. Extending my hand, I smiled, "Welcome once again to *Hearts Desire.*" I explained my being the announcer on KWCO, which had carried his show back in 1946. He really seemed pleased as Jack came in.

"Jack, this is Jimmy Weldon. He used to hear me on radio back in Oklahoma."

Jack winked, "How's my little friend, Webster?"

You could have knocked me over with a feather. I was so relieved and thrilled that he knew who I was. He, Ben and I walked across the set through the door from where we were to enter the scene.

This was the hotel where a murder had occurred, and Sgt. Friday and his partner were there to investigate. I was the manager, showing them the room where it had happened. If you recall, all characters speak relatively quiet on *Dragnet.*

Jack looked at me, "Are you ready?"

I smiled, "Yes, sir!"

No rehearsal. We were just going to shoot it.

"Roll it," he called from behind the door. The scene was marked, and out the door we came. There were some marks to walk to and stand on as I gave my lines, so I went straight to them, but I looked around the room a bit before getting there.

Jack gave his line, "Has anybody been in here since the murder?"

I came back with a firm, "**No sir! I told everybody to stay out of this room!**"

Jack looked over to Ben, who was laughing now, and said, "What's the matter?"

Ben quipped, "I didn't expect that to come out!"

A man waaaay up in the catwalk of the studio yelled down, "**Give 'em hell, Texas!**"

I looked at Jack.

"Did I do something wrong?"

He walked over, put his arm around my shoulder, and said, "No, no, Jimmy."

He was still laughing quietly to himself.

"Do just what you did, only this time, since this is *your* hotel, walk straight to the marks and don't look around. You know what's in here already."

Then, "Come on, Ben, let's do our part now."

We shot it, and Jack asked me if he could please jump (out of sequence) to other dialogue with the camera right where it was. Oh, how truly thankful I was that I knew the script.

"Yes sir, we can."

We shot about seven pages of dialogue in such a short time that he was grinning... *like Dad's cat.*

"All right, go to the next set," Jack directed the staff.

"Jimmy, I want twenty seconds of film where I'll

narrate over it. We're going to come back to the hotel to see if anyone suspicious looking has returned. There's no audio, so you don't need to say anything, just look at me and nod yes or no as I do. Okay?"

"Yes, sir."

Jack turned to the cameraman, "Give me twenty seconds on this one. Roll it." The camera was right in my face, a real tight shot.

"Has anyone been back here since we came the other day?" With that, Jack nodded for me to shake my head yes.

That triggered me, "Yes, sir, a long black Cadillac with four men came by, and they had a big police, uh, German Shepherd with them."

Jack looked shocked, backed up a bit, and said, "No kiddin'!"

I kept going. "Yeah, they were sure eyeing this place as they drove around here—about four times. They parked once on the other side of the street, and one let the dog out on the grass for a minute, like he was just wanting to stretch his legs. It was a brand new Cadillac, almost as long as a limousine."

I was rattling off more about the car and how sorry I was that I had not been able to get the license plate number, because I knew this would be important for him to have, but it was smudged, both in the front and back, with mud.

The cameraman announced that he had twenty seconds of film, and Jack snapped, "Let him go!" and I did. Finally, Jack walked in front of the camera and put his arms around me, laughing, "I think you could talk forever, Jimmy!"

He was genuinely interested in my activities, and

when I confessed I had done nothing for more than fifteen months, he looked stunned. "That's your agent's fault. You ought to be working all of the time. You read lines great."

A few days later in Herm Saunders' office, Herm asked, "What did you do with Jack? He thinks you're the greatest." I felt so fortunate, because Jack knew what he wanted, and I had only followed directions.

Remember that lesson at The Royal Academy of Dramatic Arts? Anyone who can take directions is a good craftsman in the profession of acting.

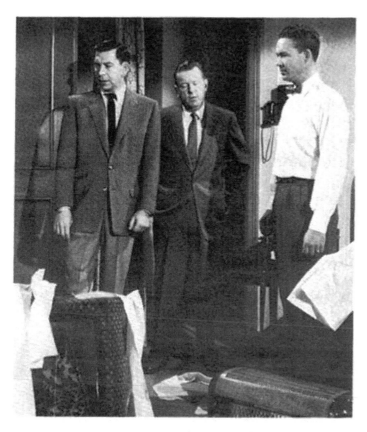

You can see this is not the hilarious opening I told you about. Ben looks like he's falling asleep. Jack Webb… Ben Alexander… and the then *skinny* Weldon in Dragnet… 1956.

23. "Patches"

Sometime in the summer of 1977, George Tibbles called, startling me with one of the finest compliments I've ever received.

"Jimmy, I've written a play for you."

"George, dad-gummm!" was all I could say.

He explained this was a story about a guy from Oklahoma who desired to be in show business, and fancied himself a ventriloquist. (Sounded more like it *was* for me, for sure.) This fellow met a real actor while in the Army and, after the war was over, had gone to Hollywood to visit him.

Upon arriving, he learned the actor's wife had died, so he and his two children, a boy and a girl, were alone. The children started calling this Oklahoma visitor Uncle Gus, and he had just remained there, becoming a part of the family.

I won't go into more of the story line, but George confessed, "Jimmy, to capture an audience, we'll have to find a well known actor as the star of the play, but anyone will appreciate it's really your show."

I was more fascinated than ever when I read the script, as it was full of "dad-gum,"... "golleee" and other words and little phrases he'd heard me say in the past. George admitted he had no notion when this might be in production. So much had to be settled—acquiring the *big name* as the star, securing the right location, and other essentials.

I was certainly revitalized. This play was *written for*

me, but since I had nothing personally to do with its development, I just had to wait—and hope.

I n November 1978, I received a call from the owner of a dinner theatre in Tacoma, Washington. "We're doing George Tibbles' play, *Patches*, and he said it was written for you, Jimmy. We have Don Ameche starring in this, and hope you'll come up here."

Would I go? There was no way they could have kept me away, but I didn't want them to know that.

"Uh... I'll have to check my schedule... uh... uh." I was trying to think of something intelligent to say. That, in itself, would have been a miracle.

I rushed out and joined Equity. I drove to Tacoma, Washington and, arriving in the middle of December, found it wet and cold. Extremely cold! I didn't have to *read* for the part, George's saying it was my play was enough for all concerned. I *was* Uncle Gus.

I'd never met Don Ameche, but this was such a wonderful experience. He hadn't changed in all these years, that is, as I pictured him from his movies.

Rehearsals were fun and interesting, but the live audiences were sheer heaven. Every night, with no exception, people came up to me saying, "You seemed to be having so much fun, it looked like you weren't playing a part, but like it was really *you* up there." I explained that George had produced my show back in the early 50s and had written this play *for* me.

One night, I was standing offstage, waiting for my entrance; only Don and the leading lady were together. Don went absolutely wild. He forgot his lines and was storming around the stage, making remarks like, "I don't even remember where I was, or what I was talking about." He was still in character, but wanting the girl to help him with his next line, to *get back* in the play. She was stunned; just sat there, looking puzzled.

All the while, we were trying desperately to whisper out loud enough for him to hear his next line. Finally, he did hear us, and very few in the audience even knew what had taken place. I was thinking. Oh, how I wished this would happen with me out there sometime, alone with him. Sounds like a horrible thing to wish for, but I wanted to do some special ad libbing of my own!

And it did.

A few nights later, Don was standing up talking, while I was seated on the couch, in this particular scene, and he shocked me with, "I don't even know what I was thinking about just now."

I jumped up off of the couch and looked straight at him, "Well, *I* do! I can tell you *exactly* what you were thinking about! After all, I've lived with you and the children long enough to know your every thought, and theirs, too," and I went on and on, walking around the room, raving and carrying on.

I was having the time of my life, remembering that *"Heah ah is, honey chile"* at the Royal Academy of Dramatic Arts. Only now, I was on stage with Don Ameche, and they were paying to listen to me, and Miss Fabia Drake wasn't there telling me how terrible my accent was. I even thought of Jack Webb's line, 'I believe you could talk forever, Jimmy.'

Don was looking at me, his mouth wide open. After a couple of spins around the stage, I sat back down and gave him the next line he was praying I *would* do, and we continued.

After the show, he came over and whispered, "I had no idea where you were going, but it was making sense just the same, and I don't think anyone but you and me knew it wasn't part of the script."

Whatta compliment!

Bless his heart, ad lib was not in Don's vocabulary. Following the play, he came out front to speak to the audience personally from the stage, and every word he uttered was memorized; he didn't deviate from it at all. But boy, give him a script and he was *off and running!*

24. What Now?

Earlier, I mentioned how you receive bad vibes from some individuals. You really don't understand why, but there's just something that *doesn't click* between the two of you, so you avoid them. It has been advanced by some supposedly *authoritative sources* that opposites attract one another. What a dumb statement that is, in my opinion.

People who constantly complain are so miserable, it's impossible to be around them. I refuse to listen to their whining; it's contagious. Yes, yes, yes! If you associate with them, you'll become one, too. I'll never forget those times in New York!

Being around happy people who contribute good, clean, wholesome, positive thoughts is normal.

I think of my old television buddy, Jim Keating, waaaay back in Fresno in 1956. He lives in Stockton, California and if I were to see him this very minute, he'd scream out, *"Here now... you darlin' boy!"*

We'd hug each other, roaring with laughter. It's always fun when we get together. Jim directed Webster's show.

With that intro, here's a potpourri about those you've met in my book, showing they too, are *still going strong!* Like calls to like, in other words.

Patti, my niece and Webster's first little friend, is

the mother of two beautiful daughters any parent would be proud to have as their children.

At forty-eight, Patti's just as vivacious and young in heart as always, and is a full participant in her children's school activities.

George Tibbles joined Muriel and our other loved ones a few years ago, but Mil is as busy as ever, flying to London at least once a year, and to New York no less than four times a year, inasmuch as George's plays are still produced all over the country. At one time, he had nine dinner theatre shows going simultaneously in the USA.

Cliff Ruby will always be productive at something. Today he makes the cutest reindeer, Easter bunnies, Santa Claus, elves, and other little figures out of plywood with a jigsaw. He paints them beautifully, and then donates them to hospitals, convalescent homes, rest homes, relatives, and others... just for fun!

He and Aunt Berniece are always involved with children's activities at their church—or somewhere.

Bob Klein is on the go constantly with some corporation, either as promotional director or consultant, and *Bill Graham* remains a bank executive, par excellence!

Ash Dawes... and wife, Betty, are still having fun, working flea markets, selling items occasionally... and he enjoys golf so much. At his age, he says his golf group is known as *the prune juice four*. I'm just proud of them for still going strong.

Moyne... sold his business to Patti and her husband. One of his classmates suggested he take up painting as a hobby, in his spare time. Painting? Hmmm... maybe. I drew cartoons characters for fun in high school, he thought to himself... and so he began *oil* painting. On my living room wall, above the mantel, is the most beautiful seascape you can imagine.

Moyne paints in the studio behind the patio of their beautiful ranch style home in the Santa Margarita Valley... that is, when he and Lorraine are not travelling. Hawaii is a great spot to make sketches on the seashore, or he sketches in Palm Springs at their condo, and finishes these in his studio. He does enjoy painting on location, especially old circa 1900 buildings, bridges, and such.

On occasion, Moyne will put some of his paintings on display, and has *sold* many of them. He has commissioned requests, but he mainly paints for pleasure. He even has photocopies of several of his oils, mostly western, on greeting cards in stores. They carry his logo, the Double L Ranch—La Moyne and Lorraine. Is he active? Does a bear live in the woods?

I bought another Beechcraft Bonanza in 1991. I land on the twenty-five hundred foot runway in his backyard, and then park it in the hangar—on their four-hundred-and-fifty acre ranch. By the way, he and Lorraine have been married close to forty-nine years. Nope, they're not all bad.

Bub... we don't visit anymore. He has his own interests now, and we have grown far apart since Mom's death in 1989. Sad, because we were so close as a

Moyne and Lorraine as they are today. I told you he was the handsome one... Hmmm... she's not bad looking either, huh?

family. Distance and time have managed to separate us, but not Moyne and me.

Aitch... alas, I fear my dear old buddy has joined the majority of those who hit the retirement age syndrome. He had planned on doing oil painting, because he's an excellent artist and would be so good at it. But no, he has become a *couch potato* and is content with life as it rolls by. Again, he's not alone in that regard.

That big name... the *STAR* I dreamed of as a little boy... doesn't exist any longer. After all, I'm seventy-one now.

In the last several years, I've had small roles in movies and various TV shows, and I enjoy doing every scene. I really understand *why* I wanted to be an actor, and never tire while doing a film. That *little boy* comes to life hearing a director call, "Action," just as much as *he* did in the Our Gang comedy film at 11... the two words, "Mine was," *he* had in the film in England... and the big one *he* did with Ronald Colman in 1954.

Whatever... I'll never stop, and I consider myself so fortunate, speaking more and more each year, to young people in junior and senior high schools!

Becoming the person you want to be and doing what you really want to do is the only true definition of Success.

I developed a four hour seminar titled *The Leader In You*, and recently was given a most treasured award—authorized Continuing Education Instructor